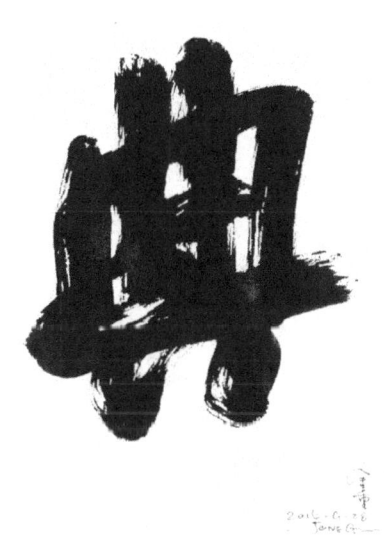

Dian

For Dian Qiu
谨以此书献给伟大的诗人典裘沽酒
金重

100 Portraits of Dian Qiu
A Great Chinese Poet

中国伟大的诗人典裘肖像 100 幅

Jin Zhong
金重

Survivor Village Books

100 Portraits of Dian Qiu,
A Great Chinese Poet
by Jin Zhong

With Poems by Dian Qiu translated into English by Jin Zhong
Bonus: Poems for Dian Qiu, by Jin Zhong (in Chinese)

ISBN-13: 978-1974312542
ISBN-10: 1974312542

Contact Jone Guo at: poetryabovechina@aol.com

Cover design: Jin Zhong
Printed in the United States of America
2018

中国伟大的诗人典裘肖像 100 幅
金重 作
美国幸存者村庄书局荣誉出品
版权所有 2018

SEEKING LIGHT IN DARKNESS

Dian Qiu has a very special identity as a poet: he is a police officer, he worked as a prison guard for 10 years. People become cautious when they approach the police, you know what it means when people talk about police in China. But when you get familiar with Dian Qiu, you will know he does no harm to you, not at all.

In fact, shortly after he wrote the poem *Sunflower,* he was suspended by the police department where he works. He had to work as a gatekeeper as a punishment. Because he wrote so many poems to reveal the darkness of the society and the corruption of the officials, his poems are banned from most of the magazines and publishers, his name is constantly removed from poetry conferences. He has to read his poems at private underground gatherings, and share his poems with friends over the Internet.

And thanks to the Internet, although his accounts were suspended by Weibo for three times, Dianqiu has won a large popularity in China. He has thousands of fans and many of the poets and critics regard him as the foremost avant-garde poet in the country. His long poem *The Detention Center* was praised as a masterpiece, which has succeeded what Allen Ginsberg has done in his *Howl.*

I have never met Dian Qiu in person, but I have known him so well. We became acquainted on Weibo in 2011 and we are in close contact since then. I am so fascinated by both his works and his personality that I have written over one hundred poems for him and have done over 300 portraits. I have chosen 100 of them to be published here, along with some of his popular poems that I translated. These portraits have gone wild over the Internet in China and many poets and artists encourage me to have them published, so that people around the world can share the happiness created by these strange, funny, even mind-blowing portraits.

And here they are.

Jin Zhong
Feb 27, 2018, Survivor Village, San Diego

典裘沽酒　Dian Qiu Gu Jiu

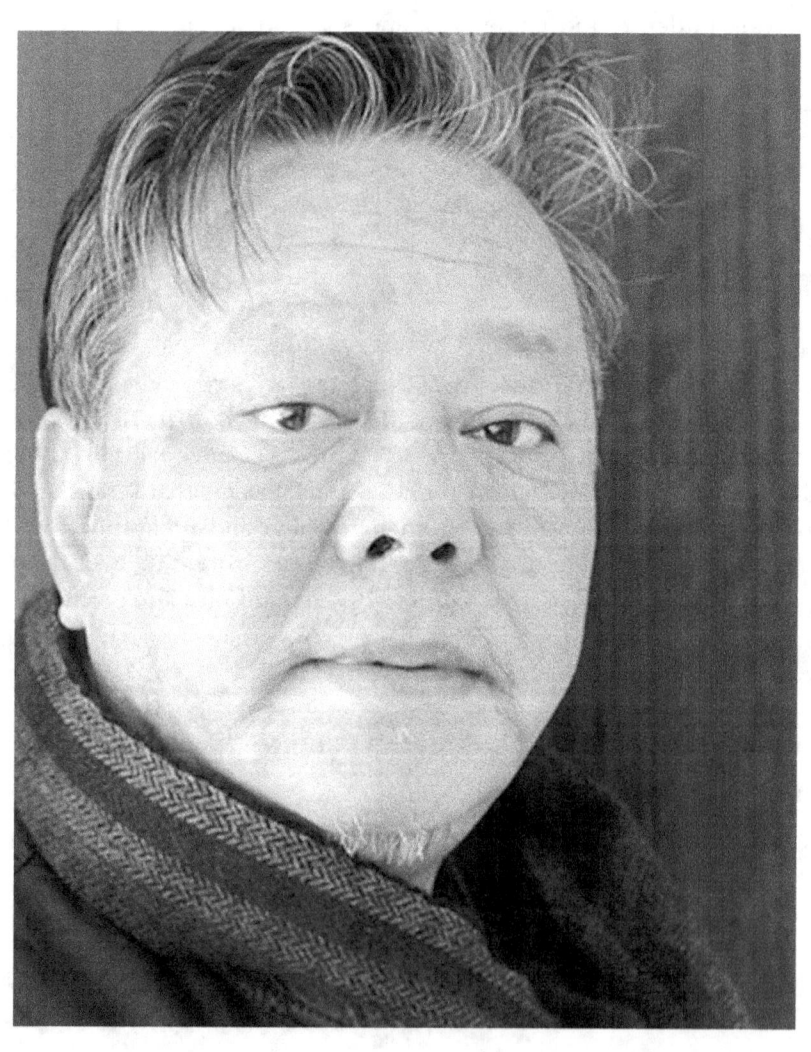

Introduction to Dian Qiu

He is a poet, an actor, and a prison guard. Dian Qiu, or Dian Qiu Gu Jiu, is the pen name of Shen Shaoqiu, who was born in Hunan Province in 1959. He grew up in Guangzhou, and in 1976, he was sent to the countryside, much like what happened to most of the young people in China. Later, he came back to work in the security department of Guangzhou Railways. Dian Qiu writes several poems a day and he is one of the most active poets over the Internet. He is the leader of the Trash Poetry Movement.

Dian Qiu also stars in *The High Life*, an award-winning Hong Kong movie. He plays himself, a poet and policeman working in a prison writing "trash poems", which are charged with political and sexual implications. The movie was released on YouTube, January 2017, by International Film Festival Rotterdam.

典裘简介：

典裘沽酒：男，原名沈绍裘，诗人、电影人，广东作协会员。1959 年秋出生于湖南汨罗，小学、中学就读于广州铁路。1976 年下乡广东三水务农四年，80 年代初开始发表诗歌作品。有诗选入《当代青年诗人自荐代表作诗选》、《朦胧诗三百首》等十多种选本。1995 年开始歌词创作，与著名音乐人张全复、捞仔等合作。2003 年 5 月开始上网写诗，同年 8 月底参加"垃圾派"。2004 年 1 月与凡斯等一起发起垃圾诗歌运动，并担任垃圾运动论坛版主，随后曾被《光明日报》、《文艺报》、《苹果报》等多家媒体及多位评论家批评和关注。2014 年典裘完成长诗《时代》三部曲：《看守所》《招魂》《啪啪啪》。2015 年完成著名情诗《高铁鹤影》。2009 年主演赵大勇的实验电影《下流诗歌》，2010 年主演赵大勇的独立电影《寻欢作乐》，获得香港第三十四届国际电影节双年奖。2015 年获后天诗歌奖。2017 年编剧《野菊花》，获《羊城印象国际微电影（网络电影）第六届大赛》最佳编剧奖。2017 年，典裘 8 首经典诗歌被收录进金重翻译主编的英文版《大篷车：当代中国诗歌》一书，在美国及欧洲发行。典裘沽酒现在广州铁路局工作。

典裘被众多诗人誉为"中国伟大的诗人"，被诗人宋逖称为"狱警典裘"，被粉丝们称为"情诗圣人"，"垃圾诗歌教主"。金重总结道：典裘沽酒在长达 40 年的写作历程中，以"后朦胧"暗喻杀手锏结合深度中国文化编织先锋语言，并运用变化多端的修辞手段，创造出独立于任何诗歌写作的世界级作品。典裘沽酒是 百年中国诗歌的大幸运。

金重　Jin Zhong (Jone Guo)

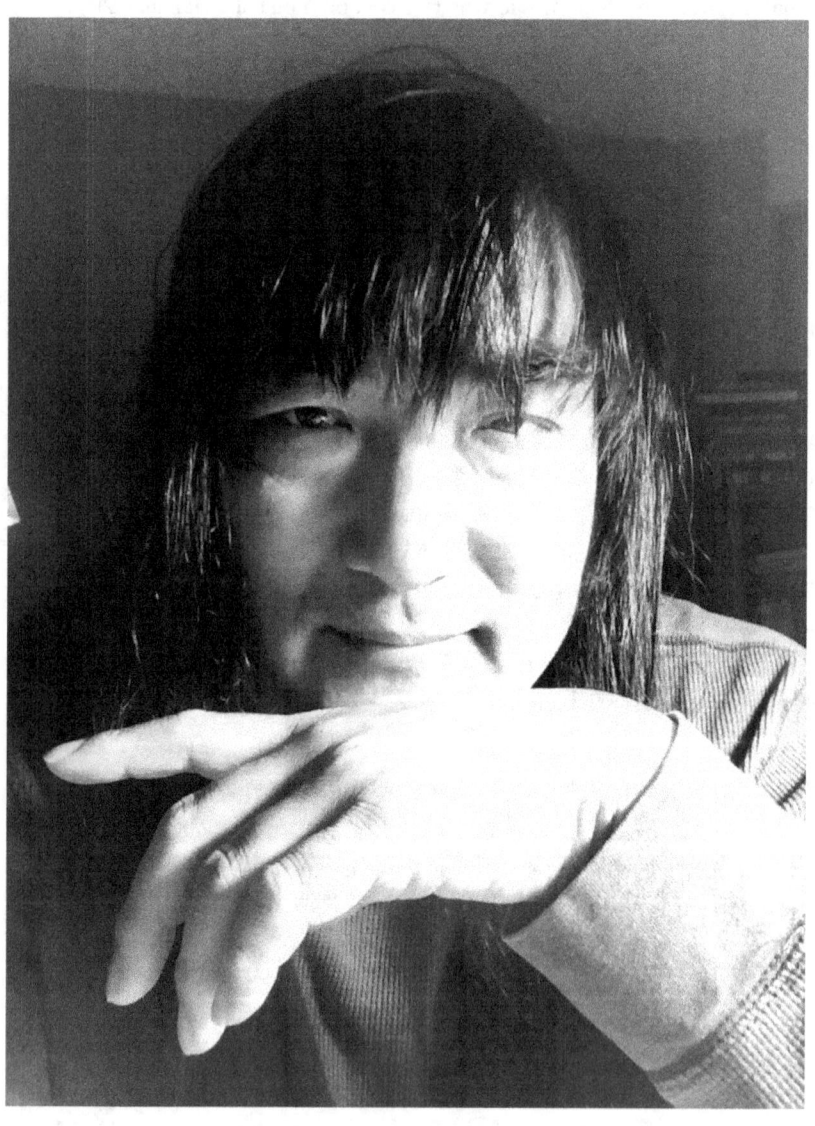

Introduction to Jin Zhong

Jin Zhong, pen name of Jone Guo, poet in exile, translator, artist, Chinese medicine therapist, resides in San Diego, California. Jin Zhong was born in Harbin, China in 1962. He got his master's degree in English & American Literature from Beijing Foreign Studies University in 1989. He was given a teaching position at the university but he had to leave China for the USA in December 1991. Jin Zhong is a translator of Anne Sexton, Joseph Brodsky, Marina Tsvetaeva, Misuzu Kaneko, the Danish poet Marianne Larsen, and many Chinese poets. Jin Zhong's works and paintings are widely published.

Recent book: *Morningside*, poems by Jin Zhong, 2014, by Reading Poetry, China. *Trees Grow Lively on Snowy Fields*, 2018, a collection of Chinese poets co-translated with Stephen Haven and two other translators. *The Caravan: Contemporary Chinese Poets*, Edited & translated by Jin Zhong, 2017, sold on Amazon.

Jin Zhong's selected poems, *Snow Doesn't Care*, will be published by Survivor Village Books in 2018. It contains poems written from 1981 to 2018.

金重简介:

金重,原名郭钟,诗人,翻译家,艺术家,中医理疗师,现居美国南加州圣地亚哥美丽的"幸存者村庄"。金重 1962 年生于中国哈尔滨,1989 年获北京外国语大学英美文学硕士学位,毕业后分配留校指教,但于 1991 年 12 月赴美。金重翻译过塞克斯顿,布罗茨基,茨维塔耶娃,金子美玲,丹麦女诗人拉尔森等人的作品。金重是多多,王家新,莫非,贝岭等诗人在中国最早的译者,译作 90 年代初在美国发表。金重在中国和国际上发表过许多诗歌和绘画作品。

诗集:在早晨这边,2014 读诗杂志社。与诗人史蒂芬合译中国诗人作品集 *Trees Grow Lively on Snowy Fields* 将于 2018 春天在美国出版。金重汉译英诗歌集《大篷车:当代中国诗歌》*The Caravan: Contemporary Chinese Poets*,已于 2017 年 6 月在美国出版,美国及欧洲亚马逊上架销售。

金重诗选集《雪不在乎》*Snow Doesn't Care*,收集 1981 到 2018 年的作品,将于 2018 年由美国幸存者村庄书局出版。

LE ROUGE

Red cloth
Blindfolds my eyes

What I see
Is not darkness

What I see
Is all red

Dian Qiu，March 1, 2018
Translated by Jin Zhong

红

红布遮住眼睛
看到的，并不是黑暗
而是一片红

典裘沽酒 2018，3，1

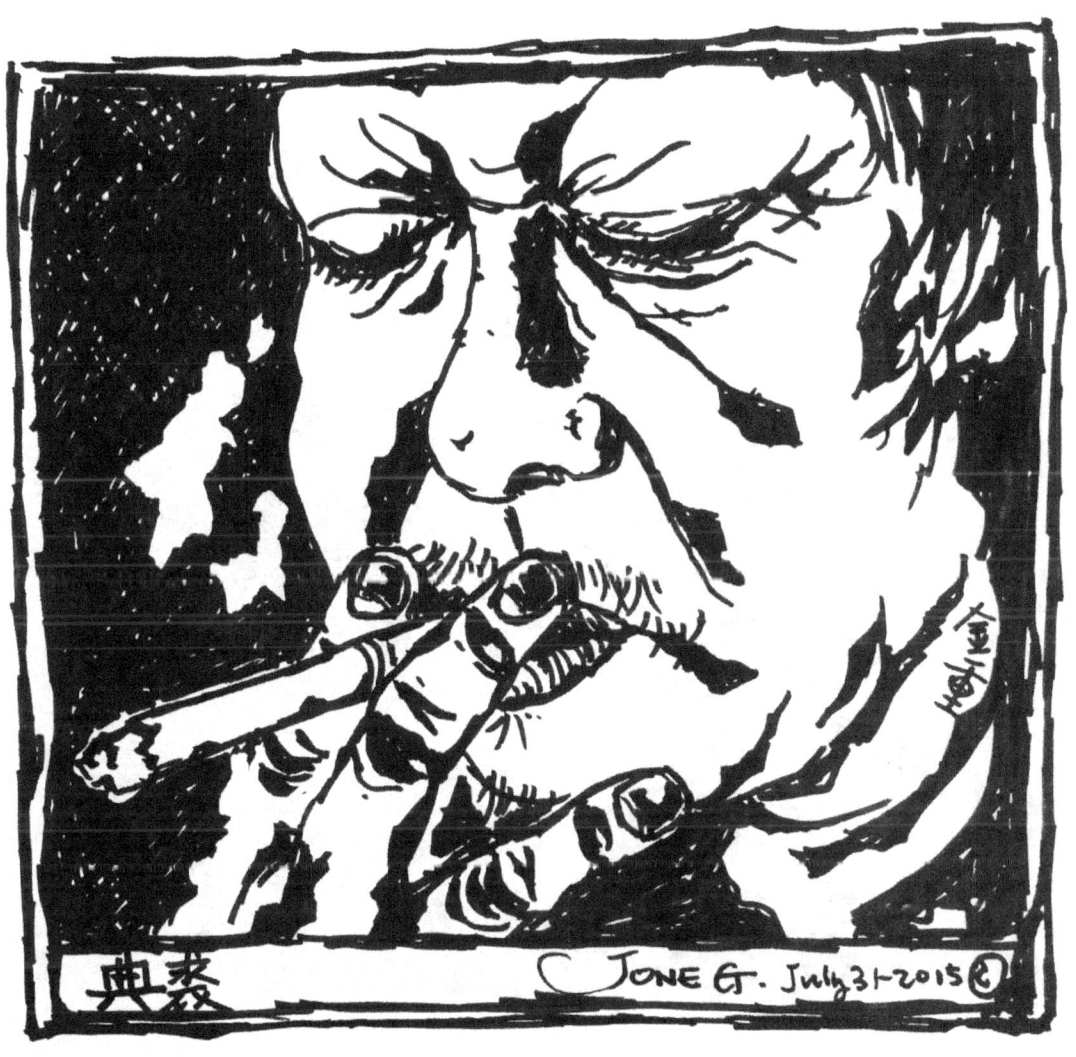

Dian Qiu, leader of the "Trash Poetry"

Do the opposite
Do the sweeping
--Dian Qiu

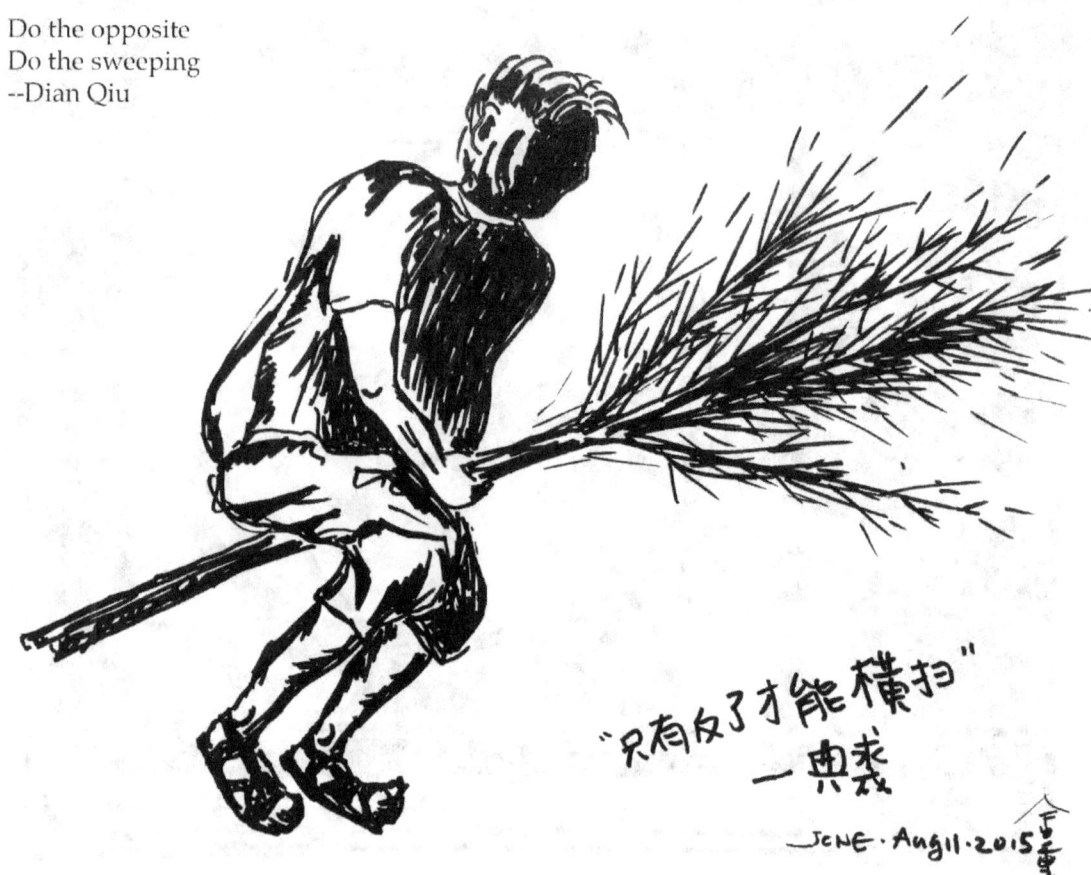

"只有反了才能横扫"
——奥裁
JCNE·Aug11·2015

典裘沽酒

虎

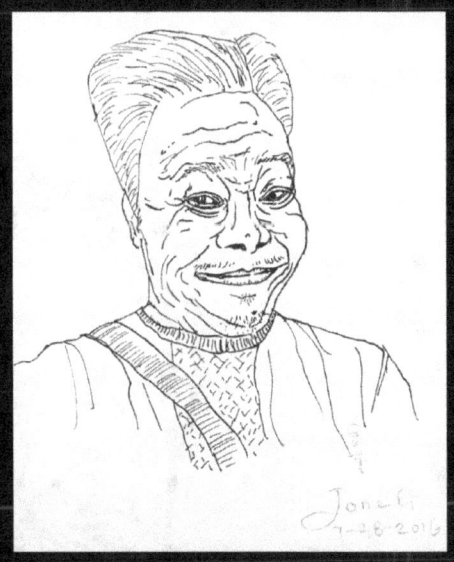

TIGER

This morning I
Went into a zoo
And saw a tiger
The Siberian kind

Shuffling from this end
Of the cage to the other end
And from the other end
Back to this end

This afternoon I
Walked out of the zoo
When I passed the tiger
I saw it

Shuffling from this end
Of the cage to the other end
And from the other end
Back to this end

Dian Qiu
translated by Jin Zhong

上午，我走进动物园
看见一只东北虎

从笼子这头
走到笼子那头
又从笼子那头
走回笼子这头

下午，我走出动物园
路过又看见它

从笼子这头
走到笼子那头
又从笼子那头
走回笼子这头

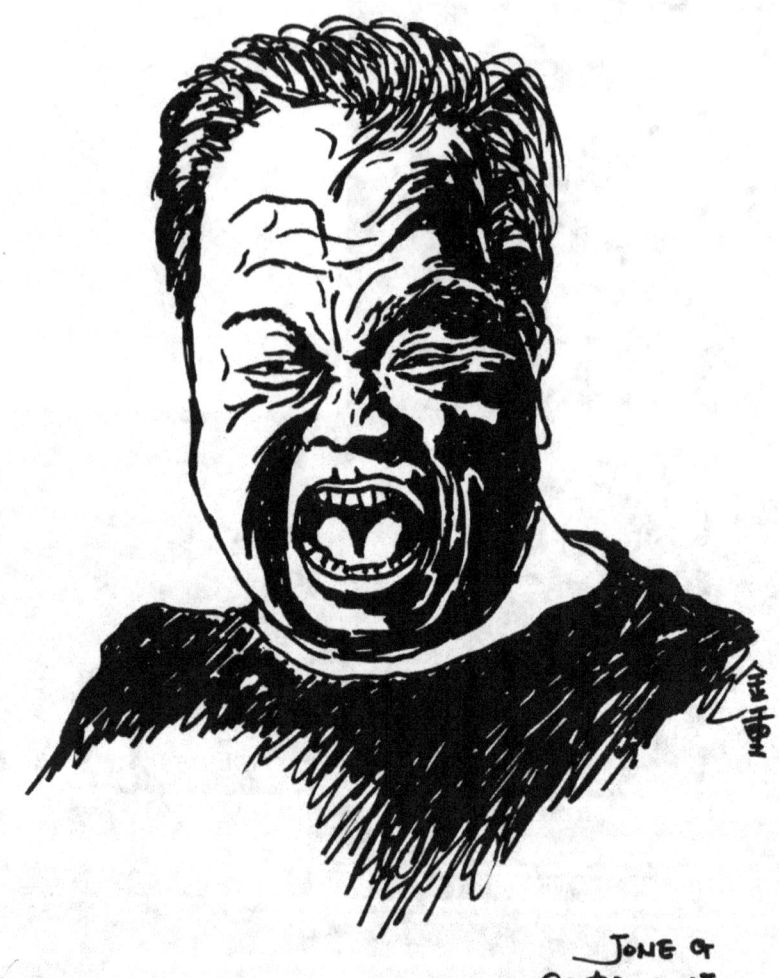

"我再次申明 我是一个热爱生命的人"
典裘
2008-8

金重

JONE Q
Sept 2-2015

Again I declare, I am someone who loves life --Dian Qiu

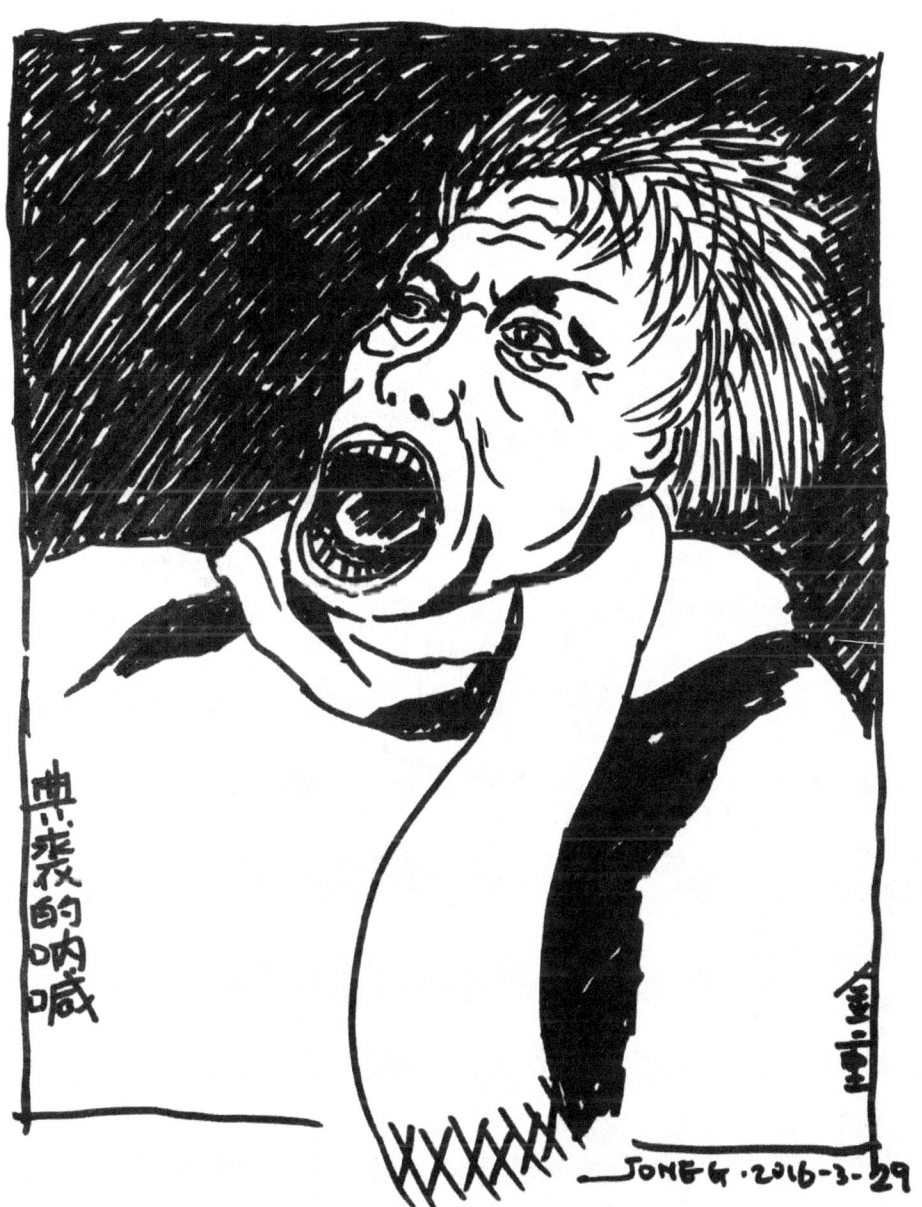

典裘的吶喊

金重

JONE G · 2016-3-29

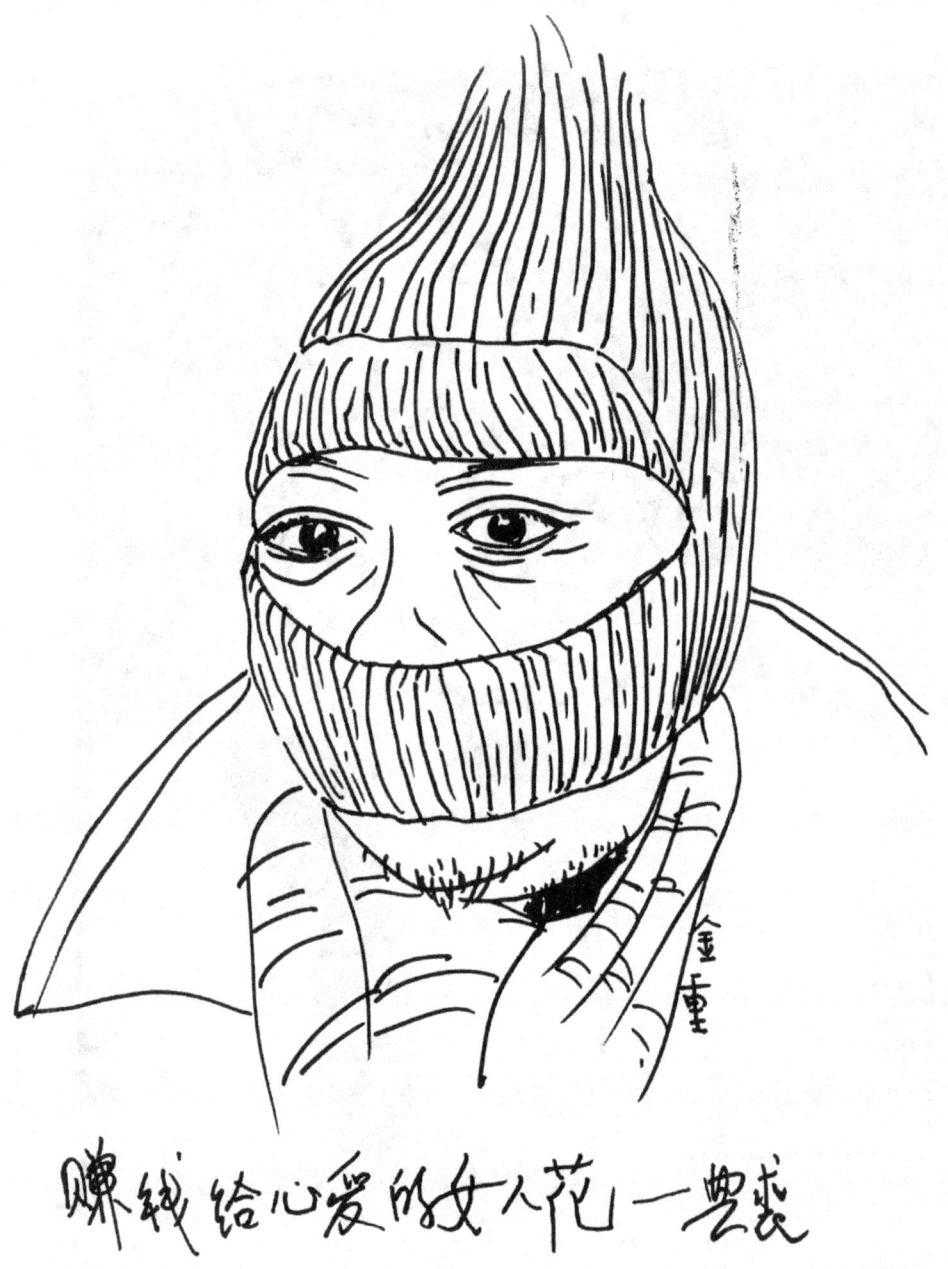

赚钱给心爱的女人花一些钱

Jone G
1-26-2016

I make money for my lady -- Dian Qiu

So cold--
A cold smile appears
On everyone's face
In this contry
--Dian Qiu

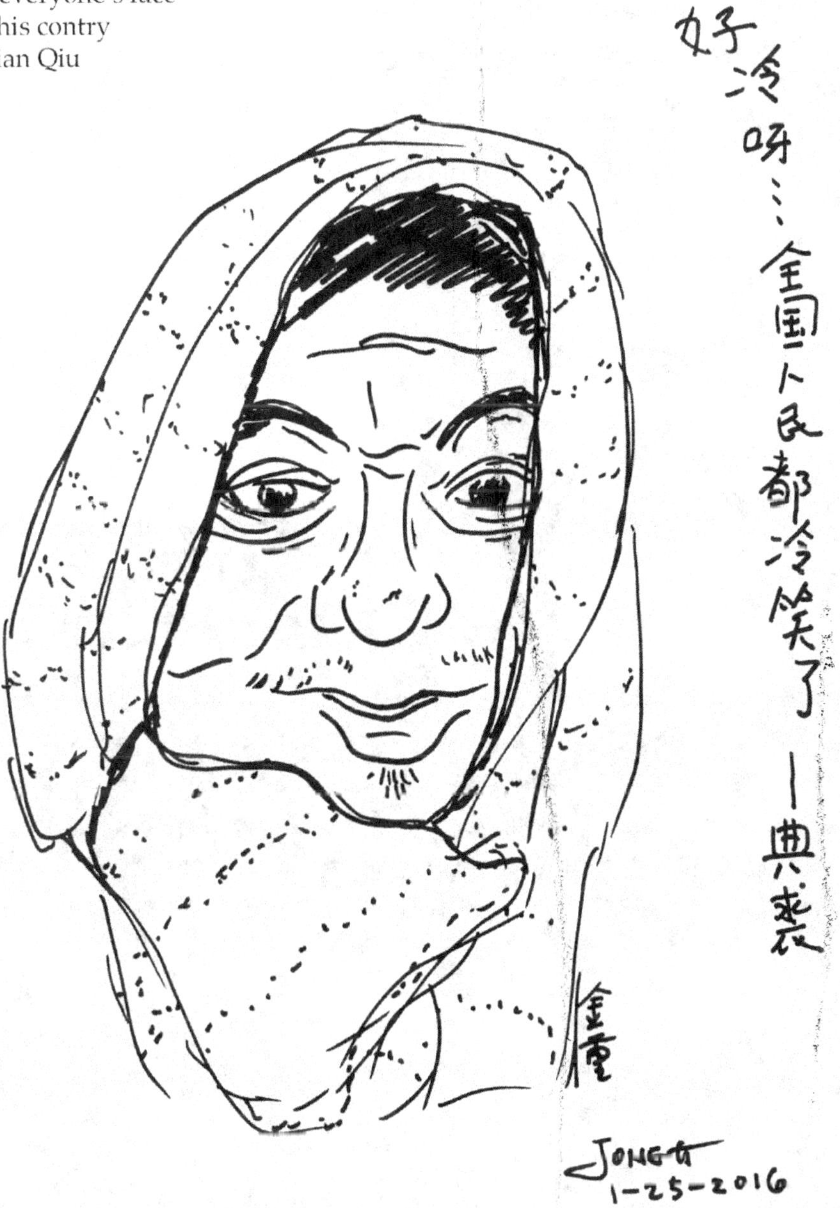

好冷呀：全国人民都冷笑了 ——典求

金重

JONG重
1-25-2016

大海

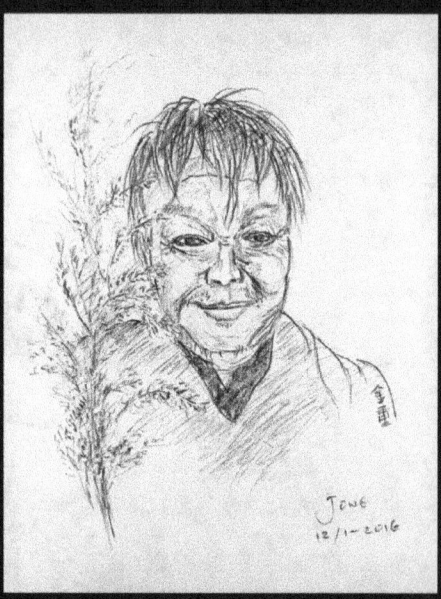

你穿过我弯曲的愁肠，推开门
大海在扬波

水手，可以死在海上
海鸥，不能死在天空
我懂得看云怎样散去时
你的背影，落叶纷纷

典裘沽酒

THE OCEAN

You went through the winding passages
Of my sorrowful heart
Then opened my door
The ocean surged up

Sailors could die out at sea
But seagulls shall not die in the sky
Now I know how to see this:
When the clouds disperse
Your figure
Departs like falling leaves

Dian Qiu
Translated by Jin Zhong

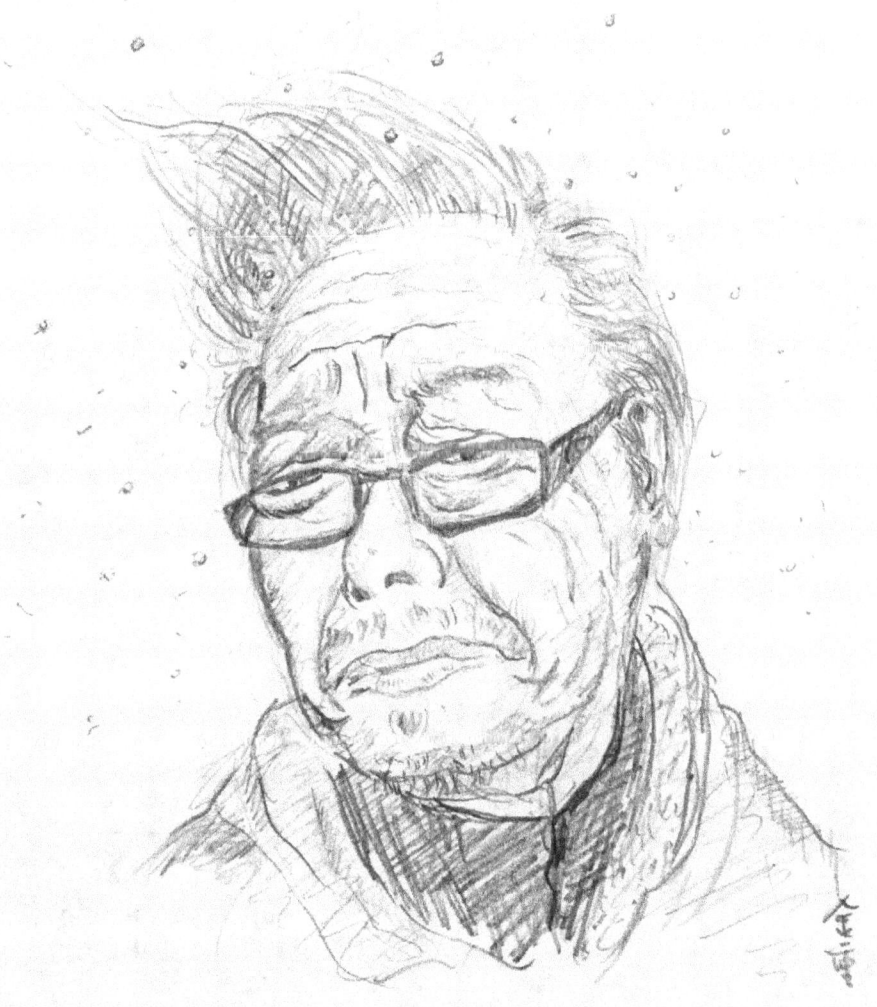

微号被禁转，禁赞，禁评的老曲。
Joneng
2-28-2016

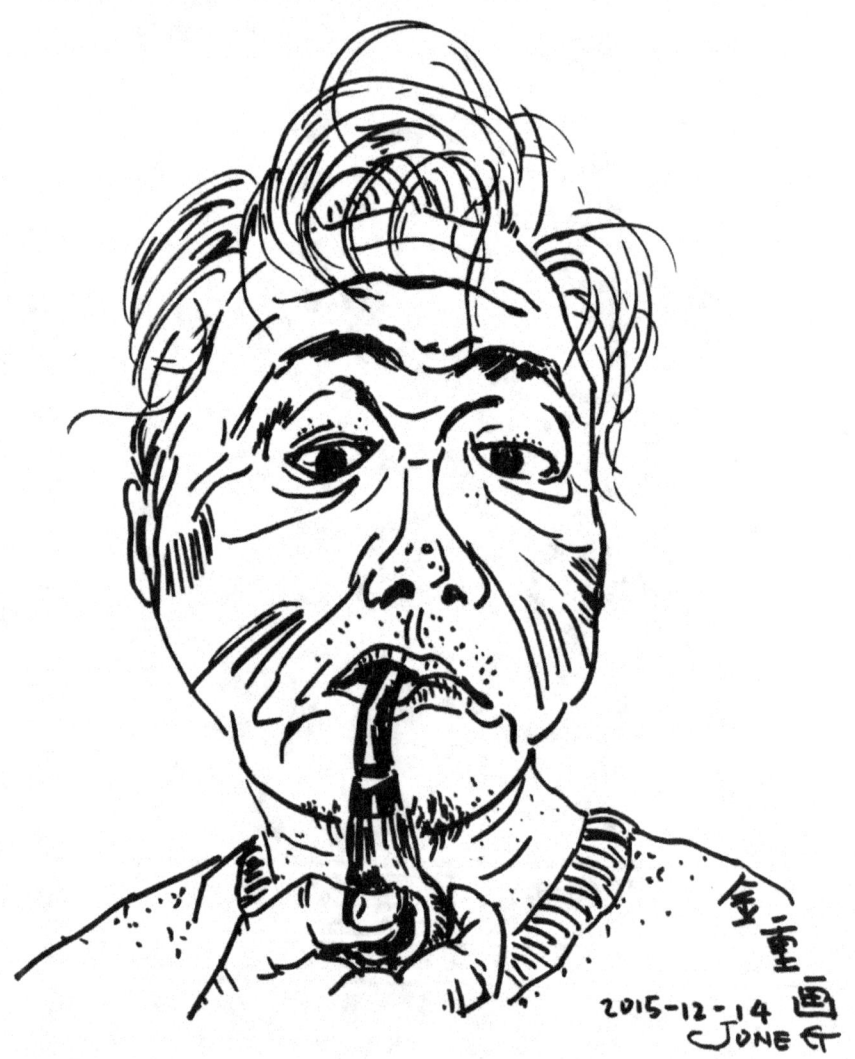

"男诗人·总要有个他爱的女人·管管·有好处"
　　　　　一典裘

A man poet　　Always needs some TLC　　From the woman he loves
　　　　It works out good -- Dian Qiu

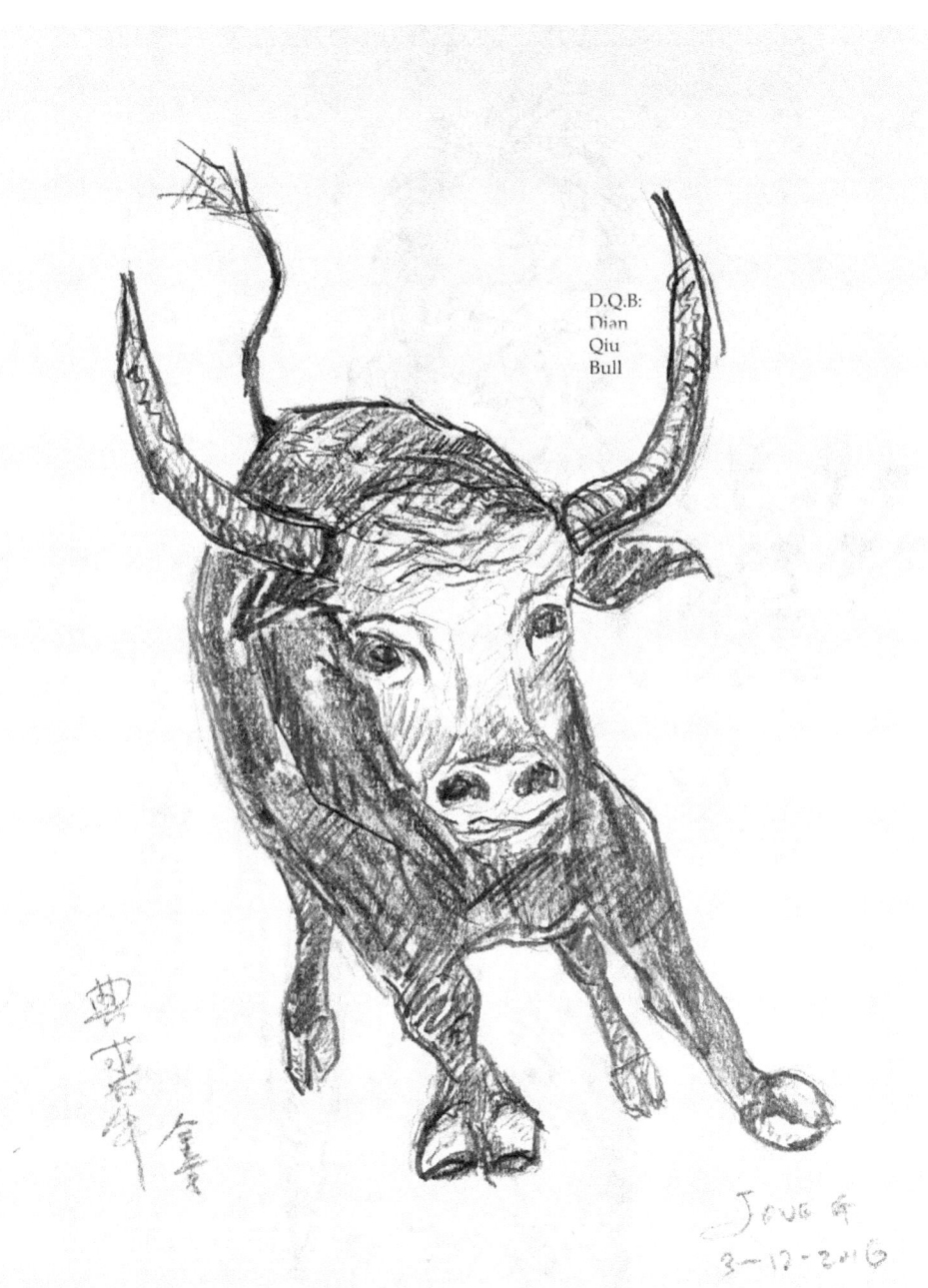

D.Q.B:
Dian
Qiu
Bull

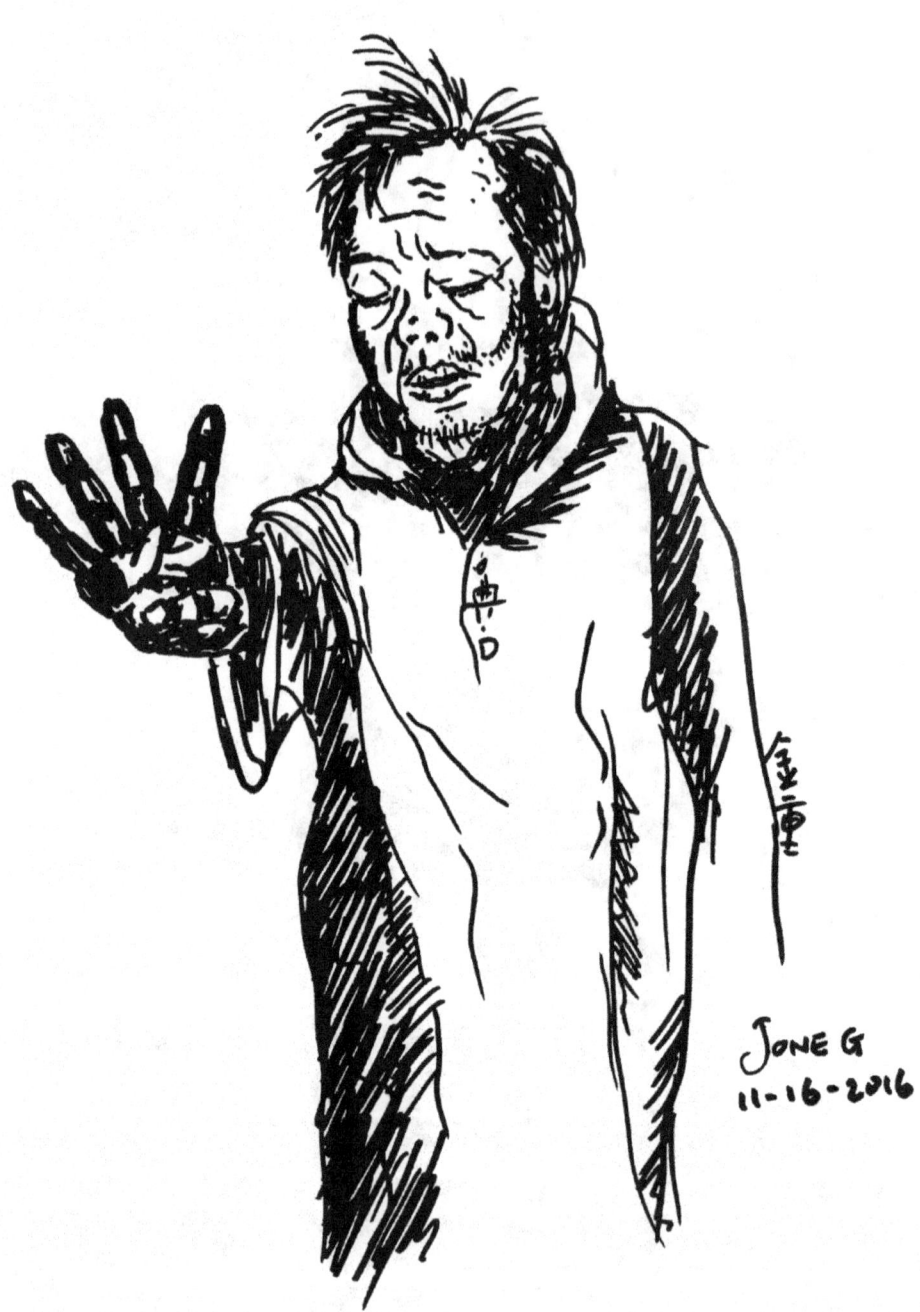

JONE G
11-16-2016

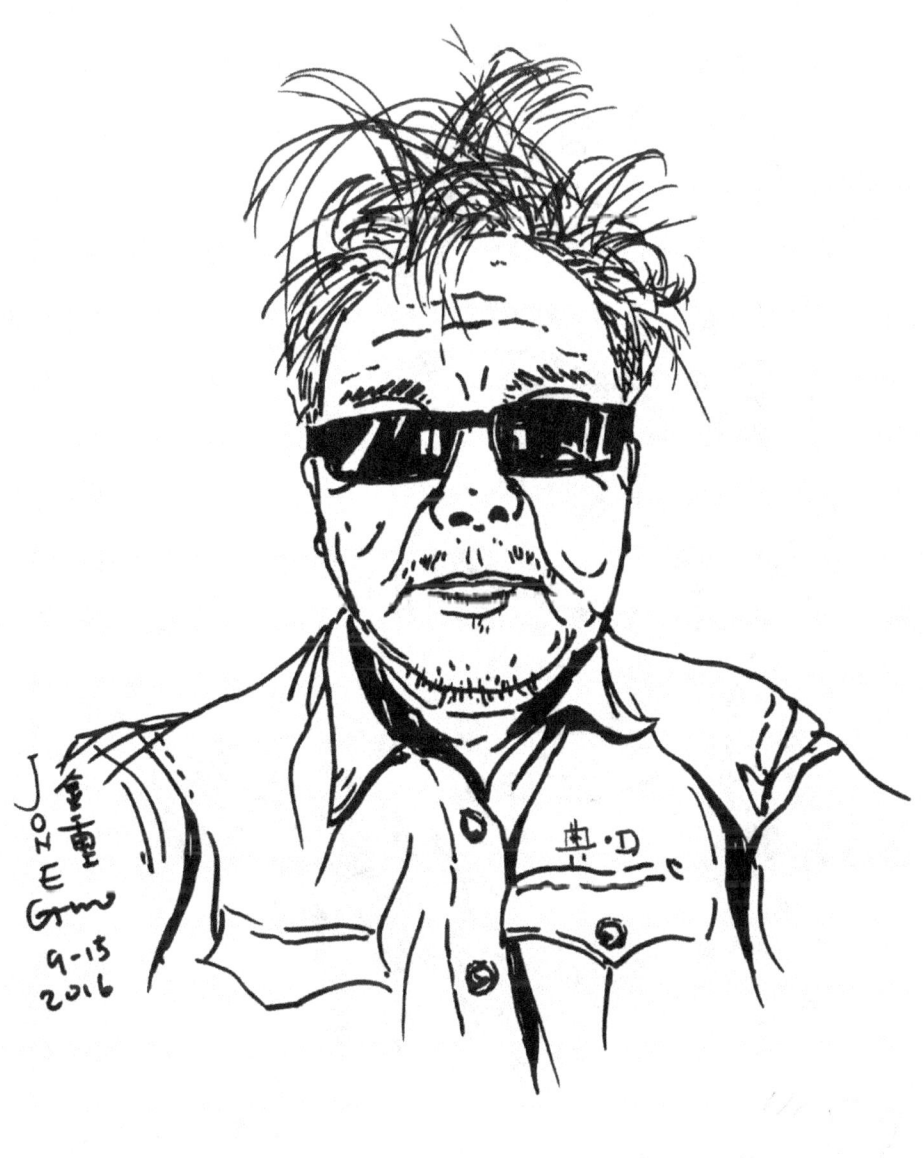

Dian Qiu in police uniform

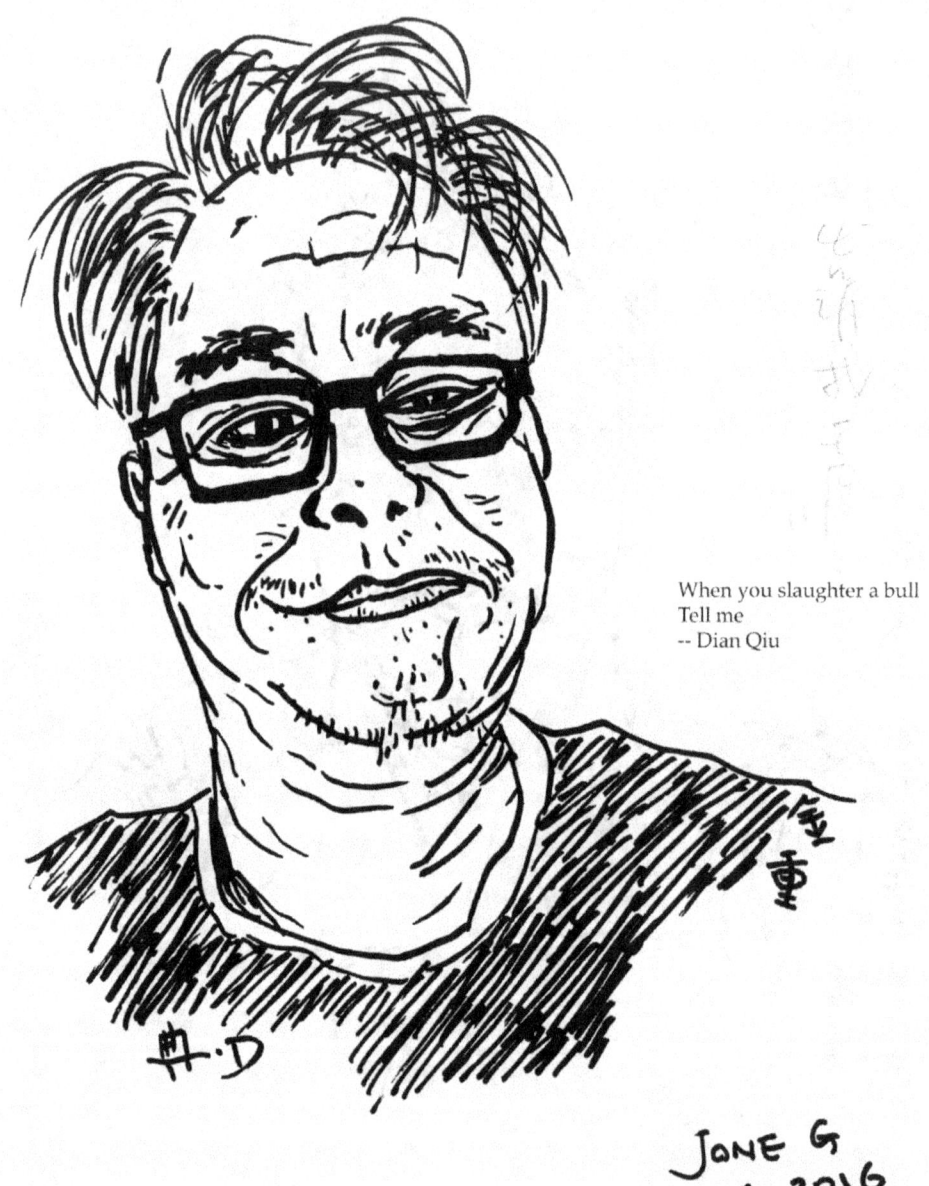

When you slaughter a bull
Tell me
-- Dian Qiu

JaNE G
9-17-2016

14

DQP:
Dian
Qiu
Pig

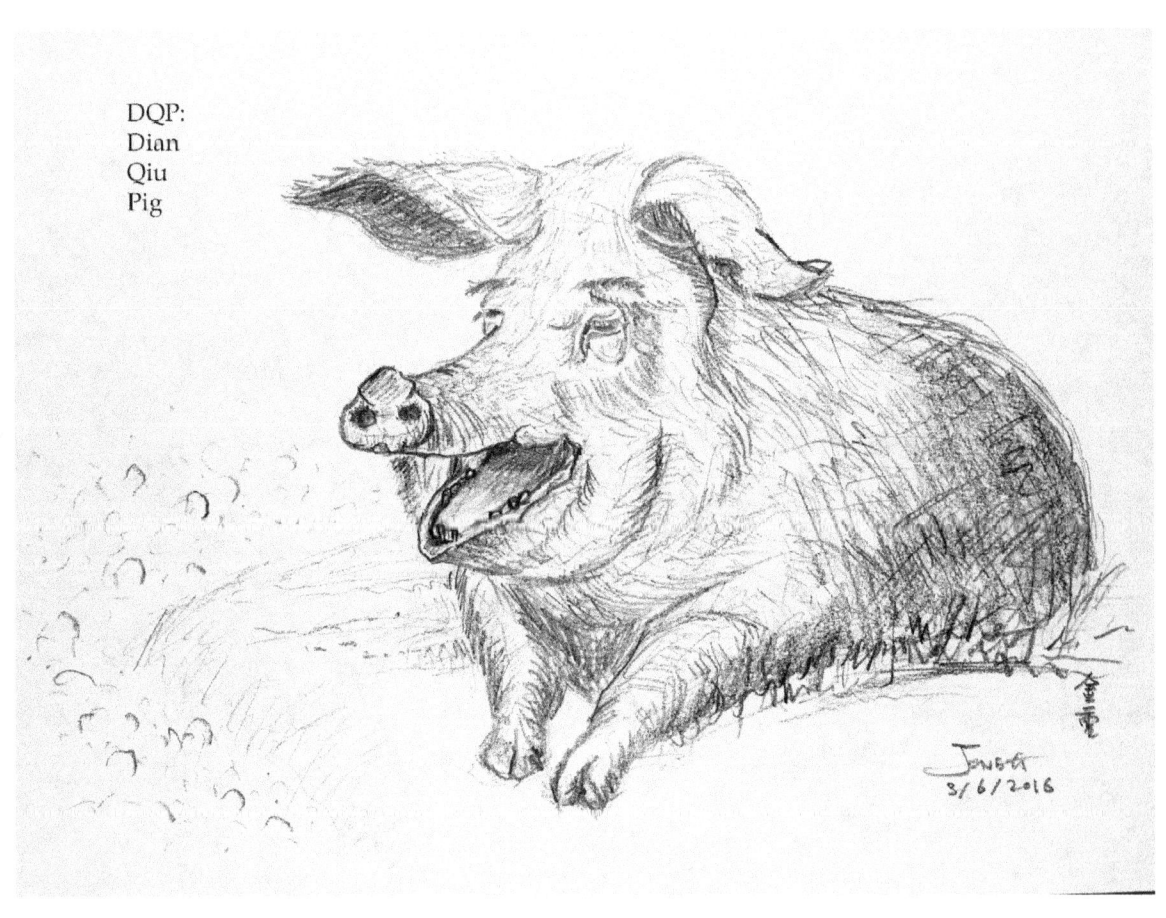

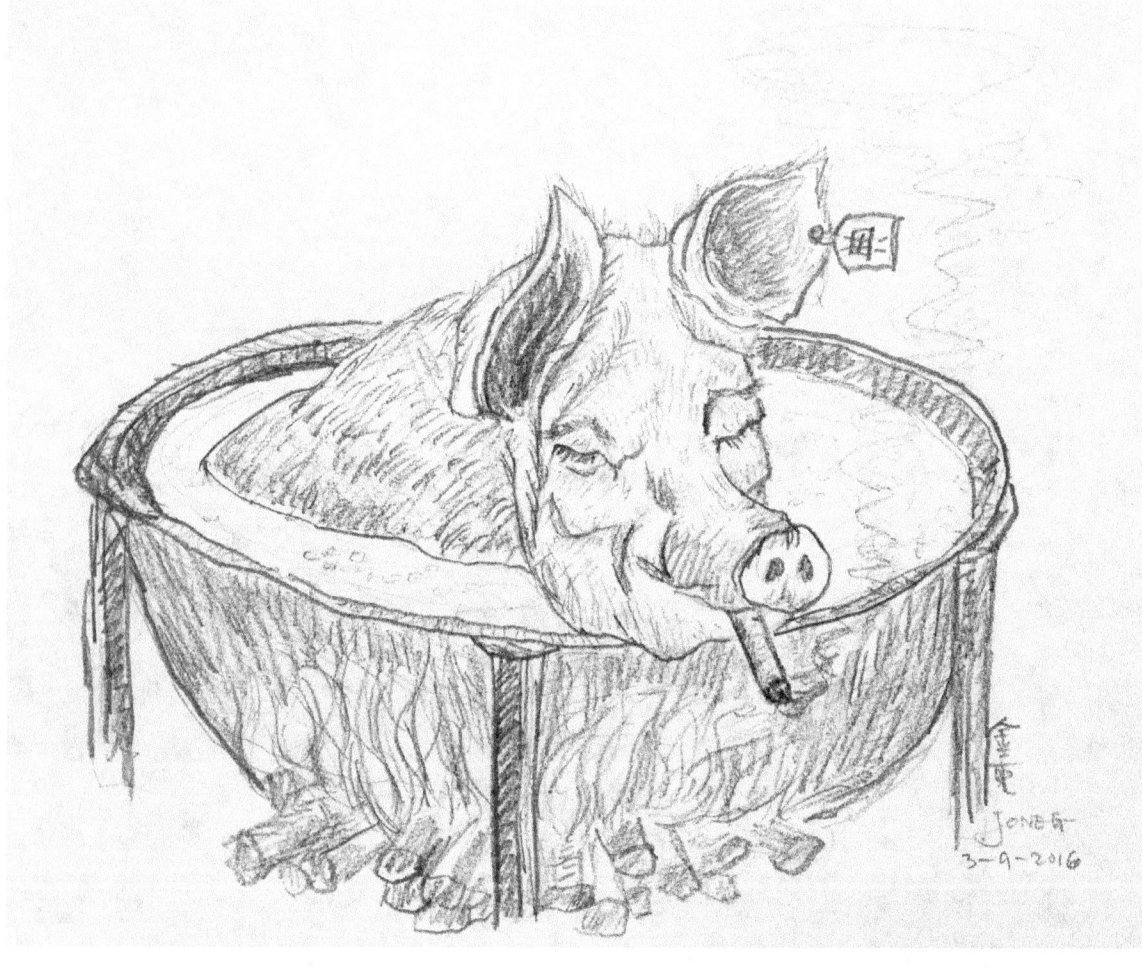

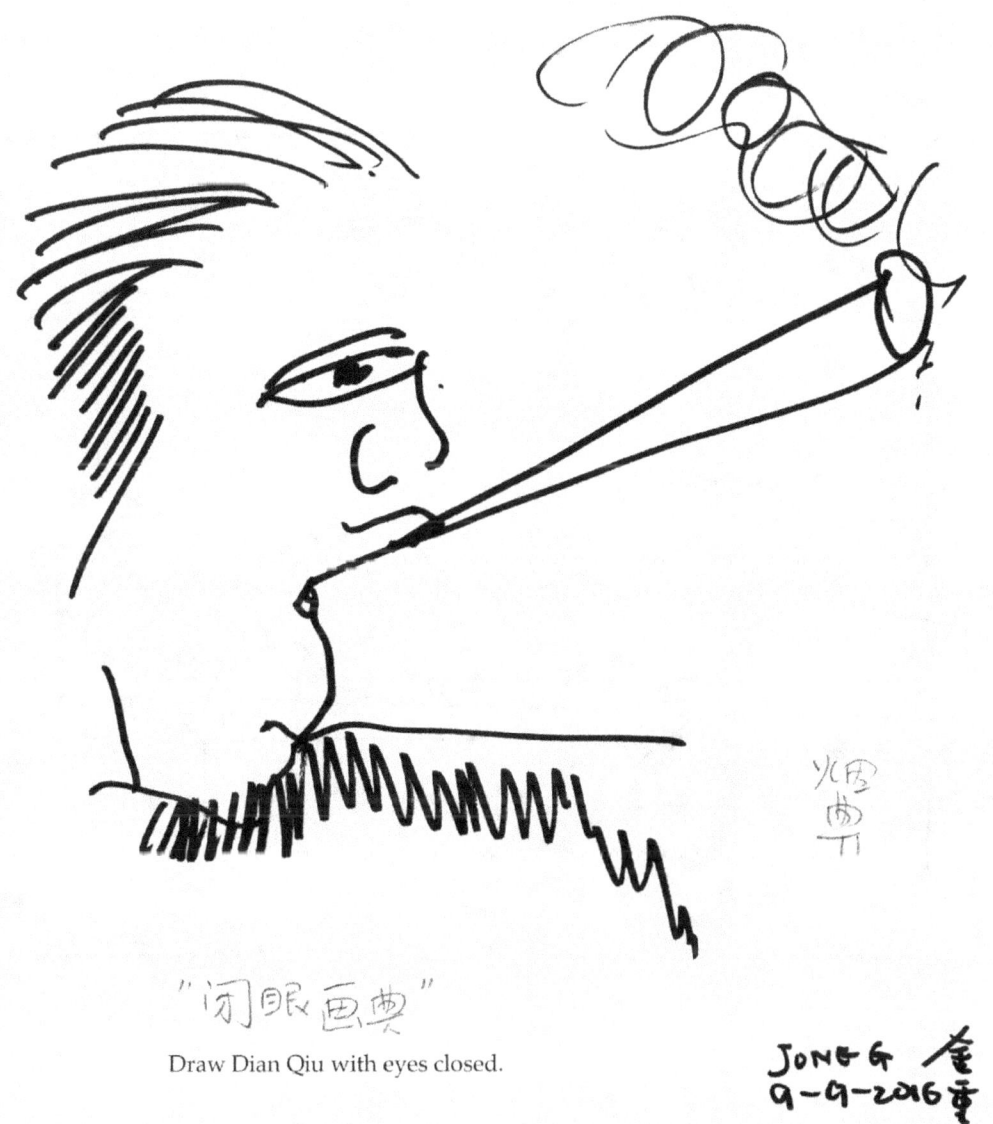

"闭眼画卖"

Draw Dian Qiu with eyes closed.

JONG G 金
9-9-2016 董

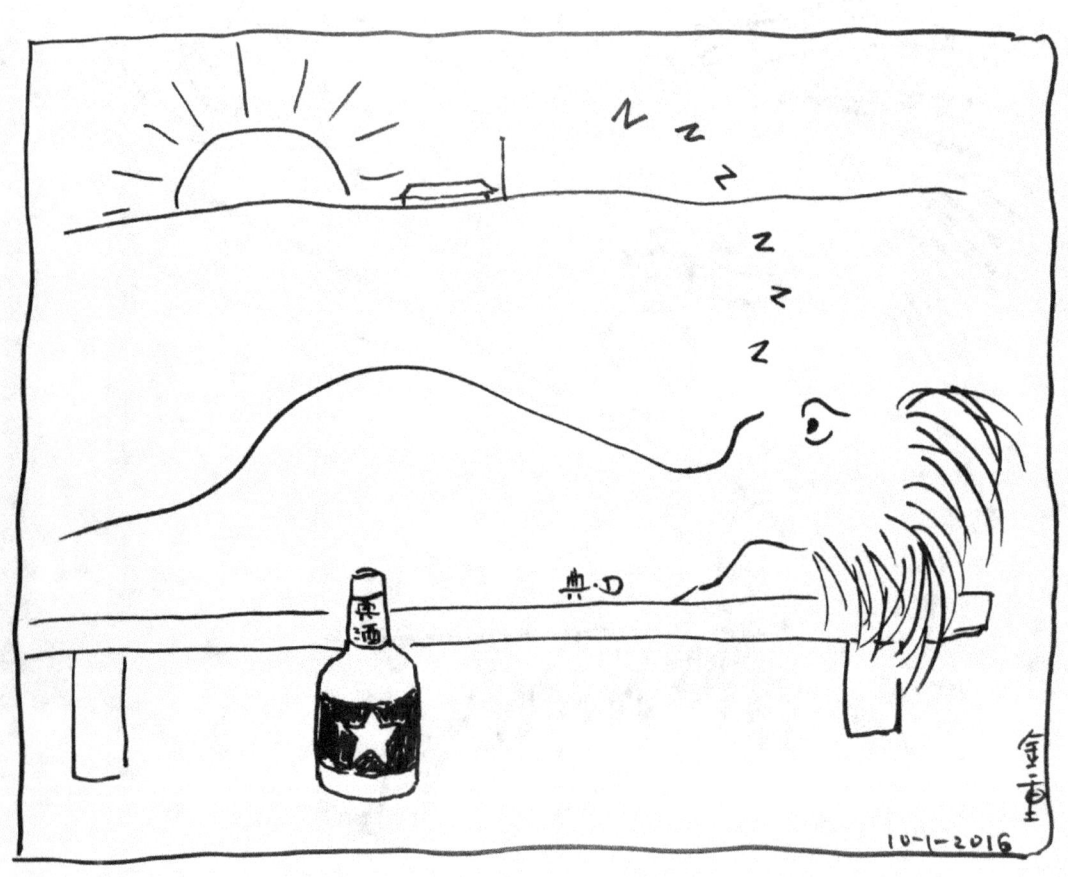

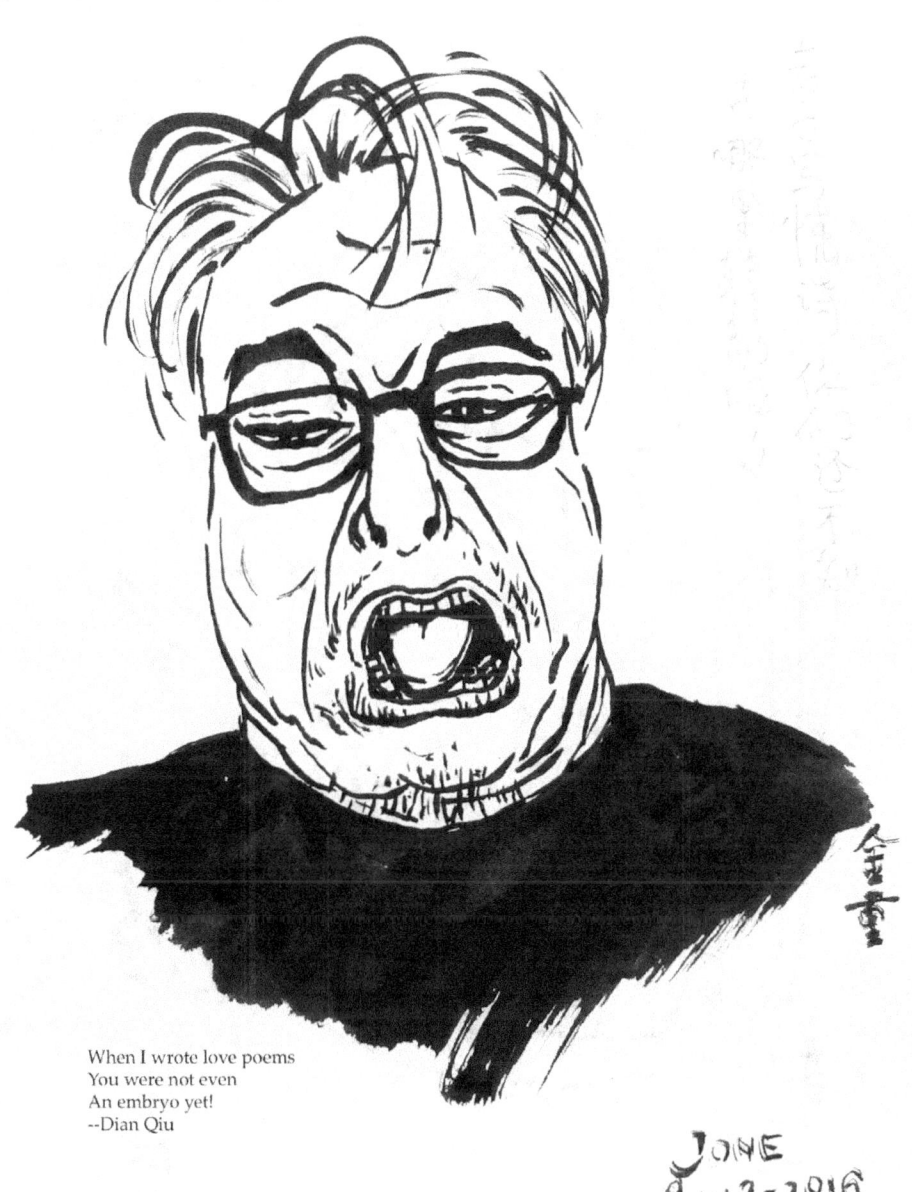

When I wrote love poems
You were not even
An embryo yet!
--Dian Qiu

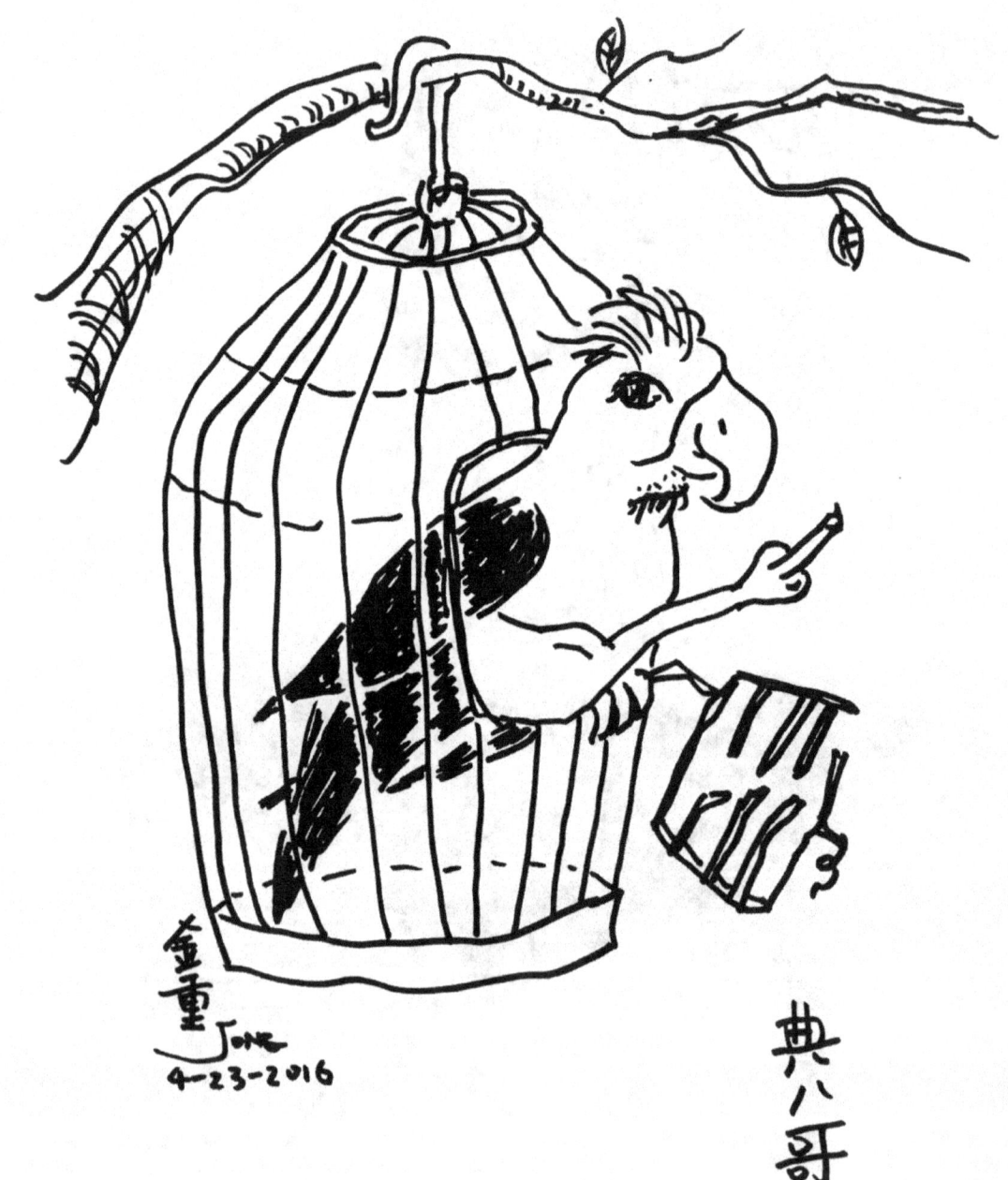

金重 Jong
4-23-2016

典八哥

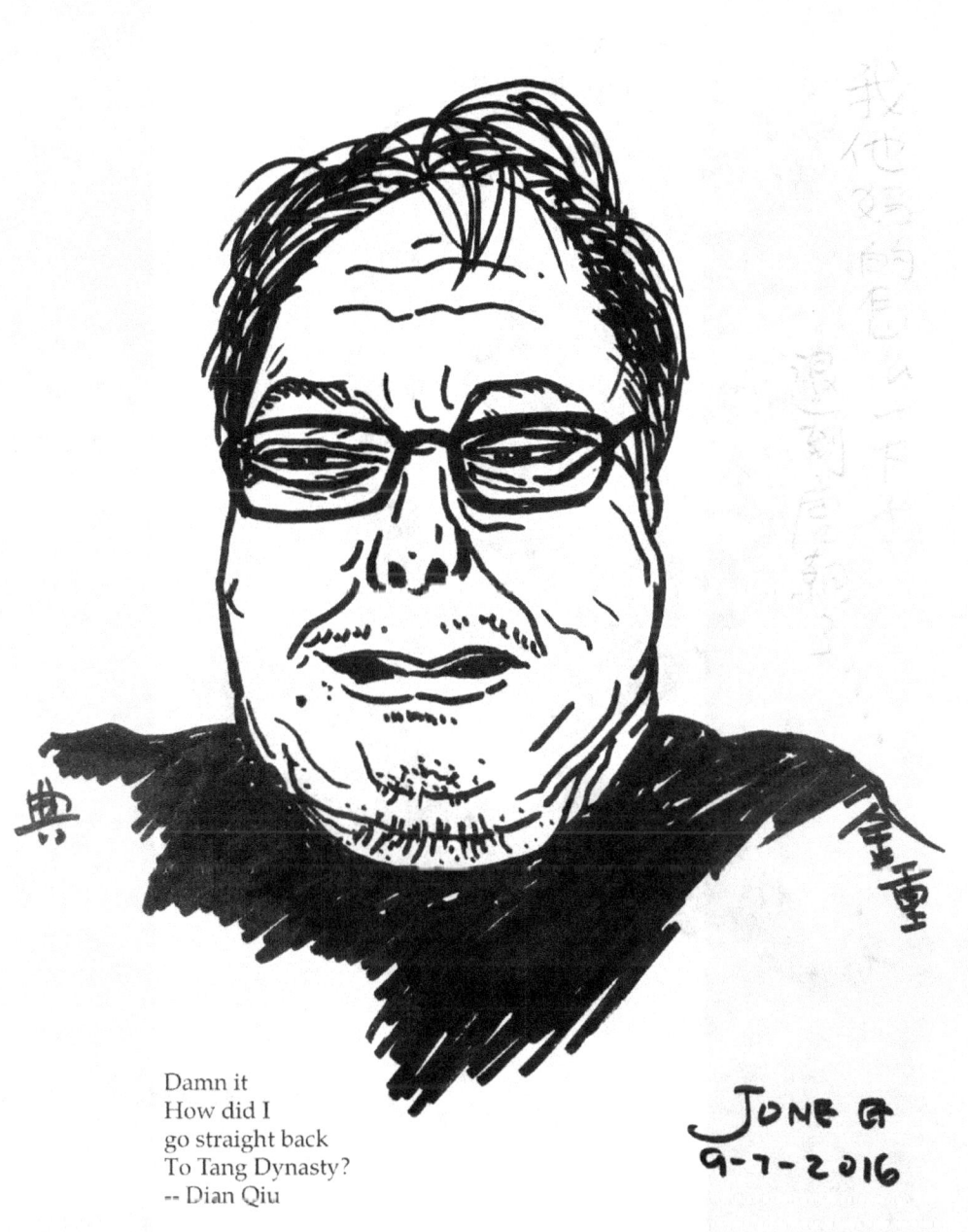

Damn it
How did I
go straight back
To Tang Dynasty?
-- Dian Qiu

JONE
9-7-2016

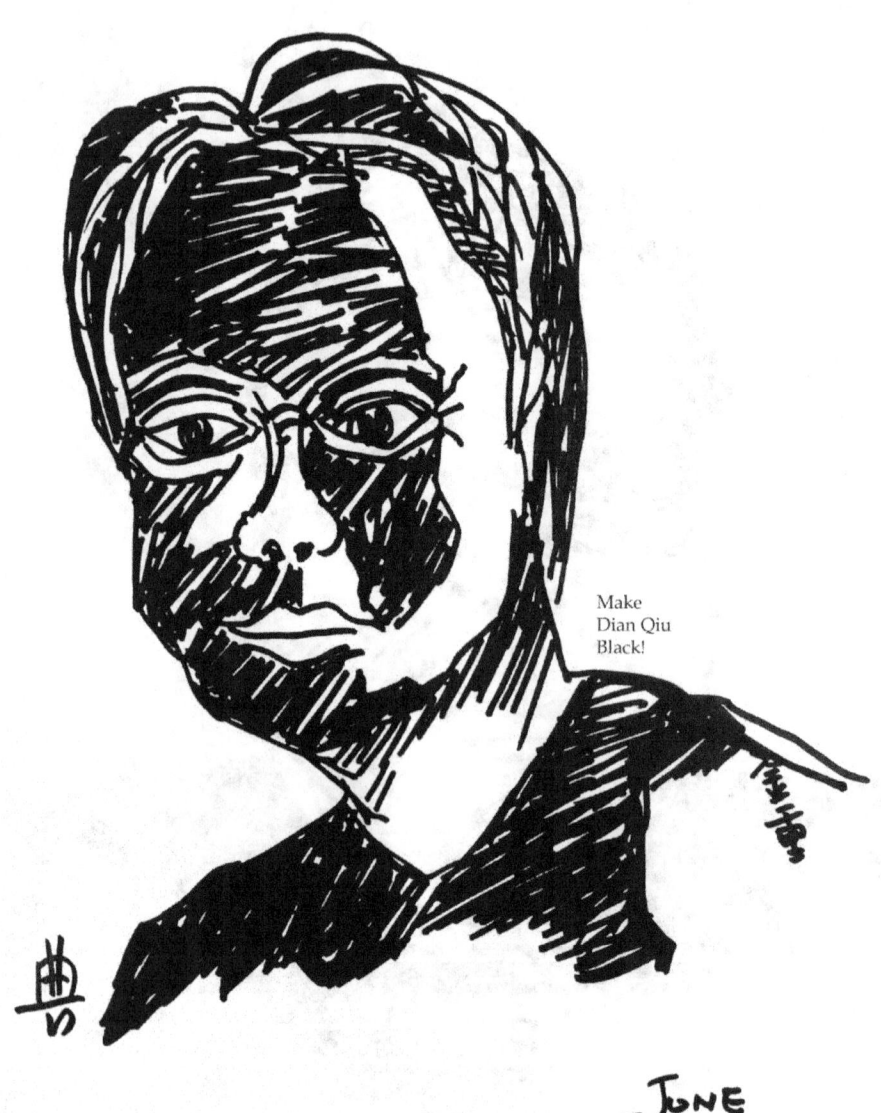

Make
Dian Qiu
Black!

JUNE
9-7-2016

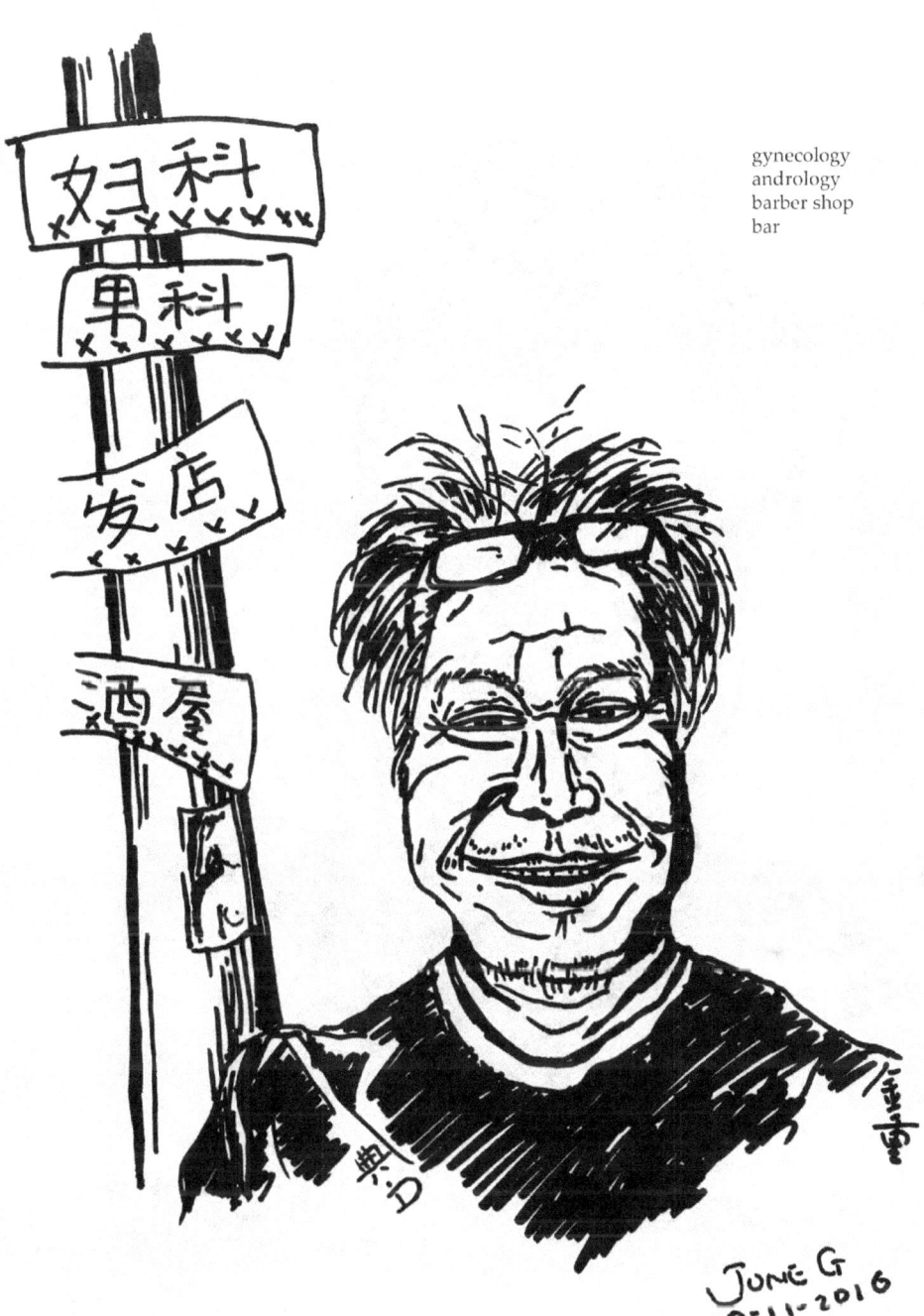

gynecology
andrology
barber shop
bar

JUNE G
10-11-2016

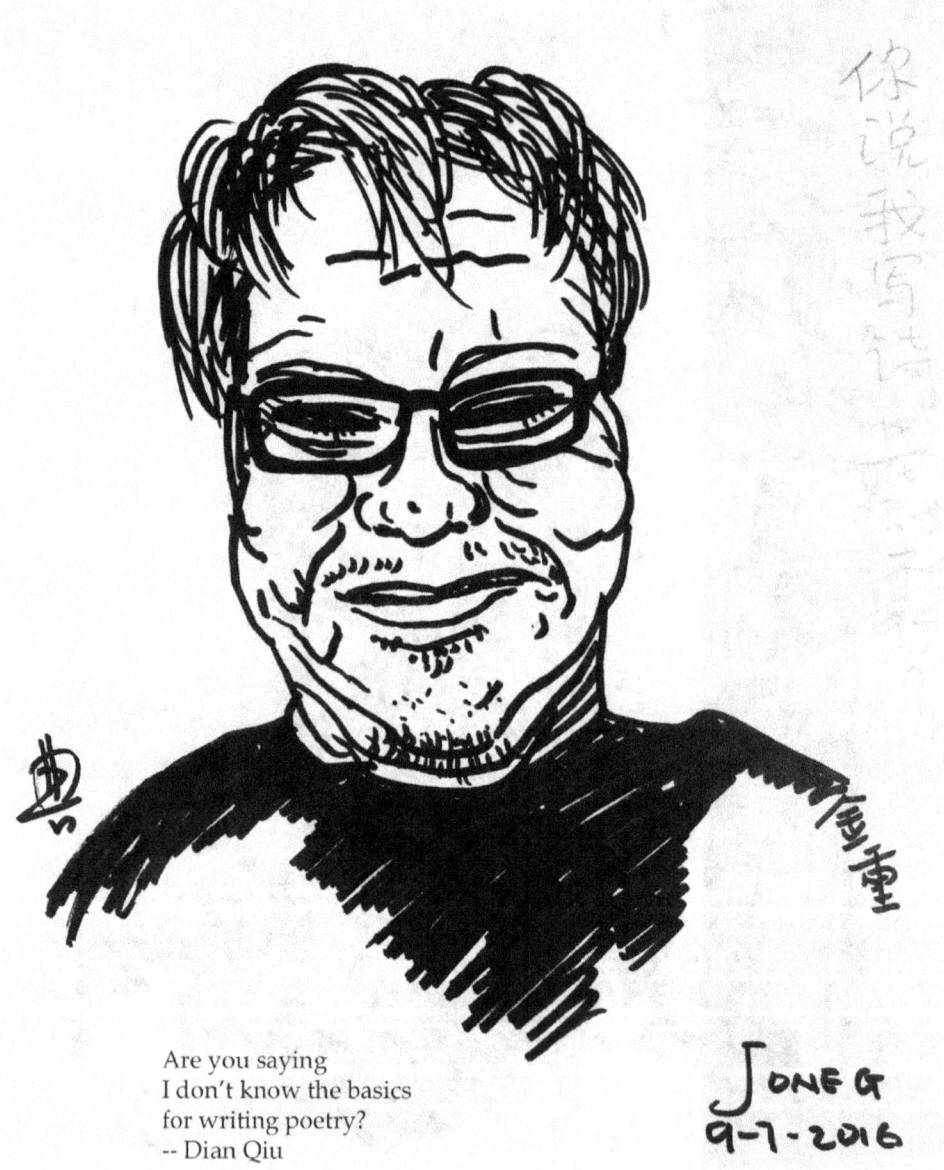

你说我写诗不懂行吗

惩重

Are you saying
I don't know the basics
for writing poetry?
-- Dian Qiu

JONE G
9-7-2016

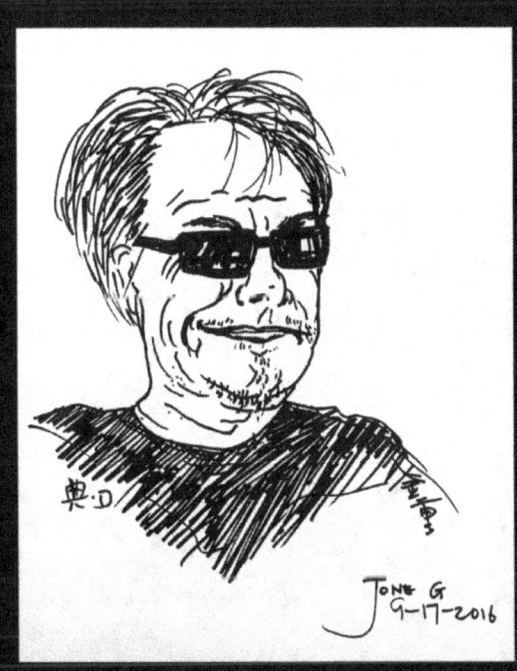

向日葵

典裴沽酒

我的一生
都在把光明追求
可我一成熟
就要拧断我的头

SUNFLOWER

I pursue light
For all my life

When I grow big enough
They will twist my head off

Dian Qiu
Translated by Jin Zhong

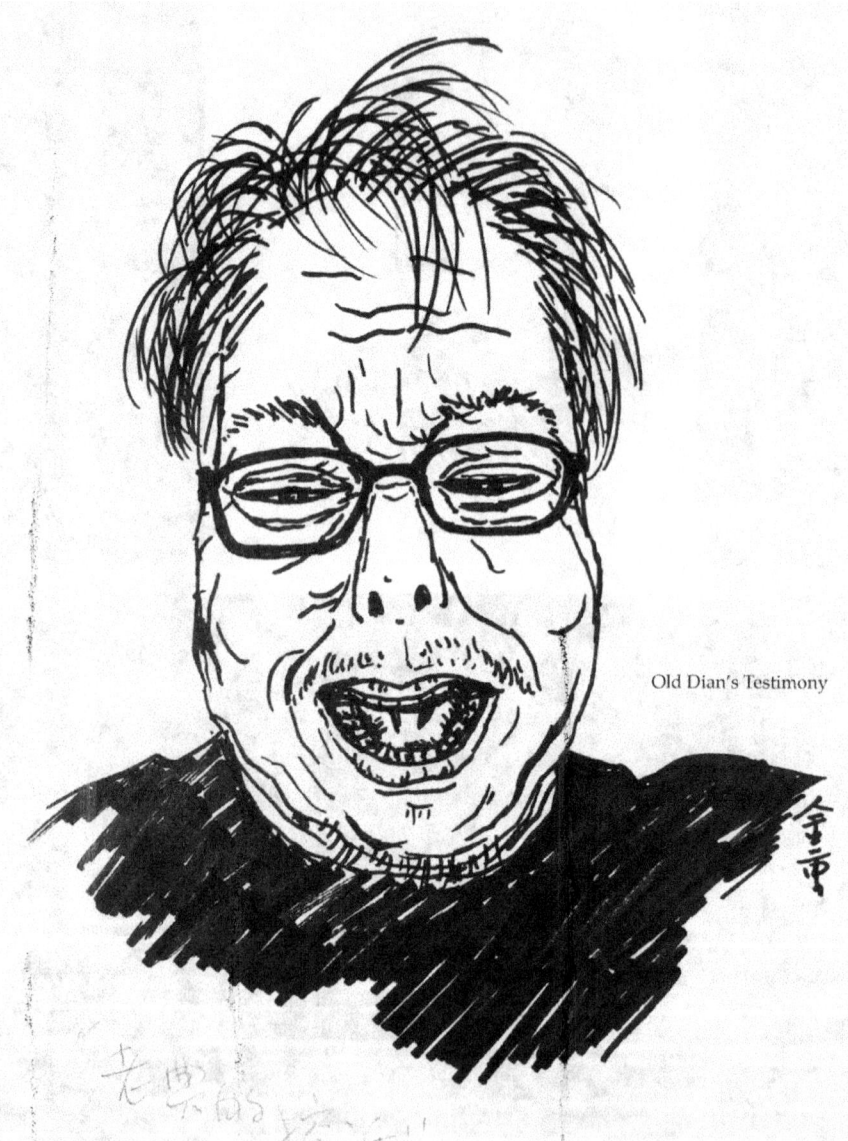

Old Dian's Testimony

JONE G
911 — 2016

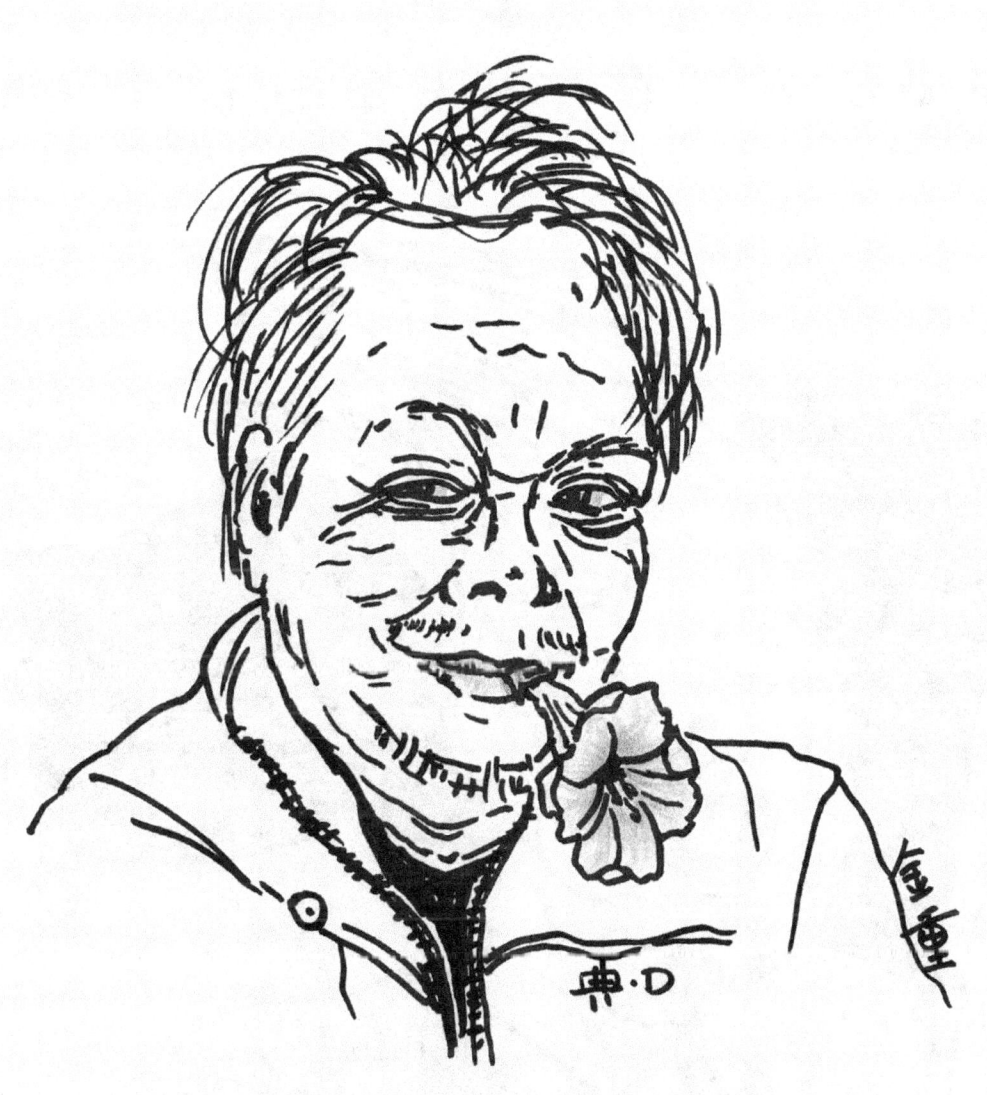

JONE
2/20/2017

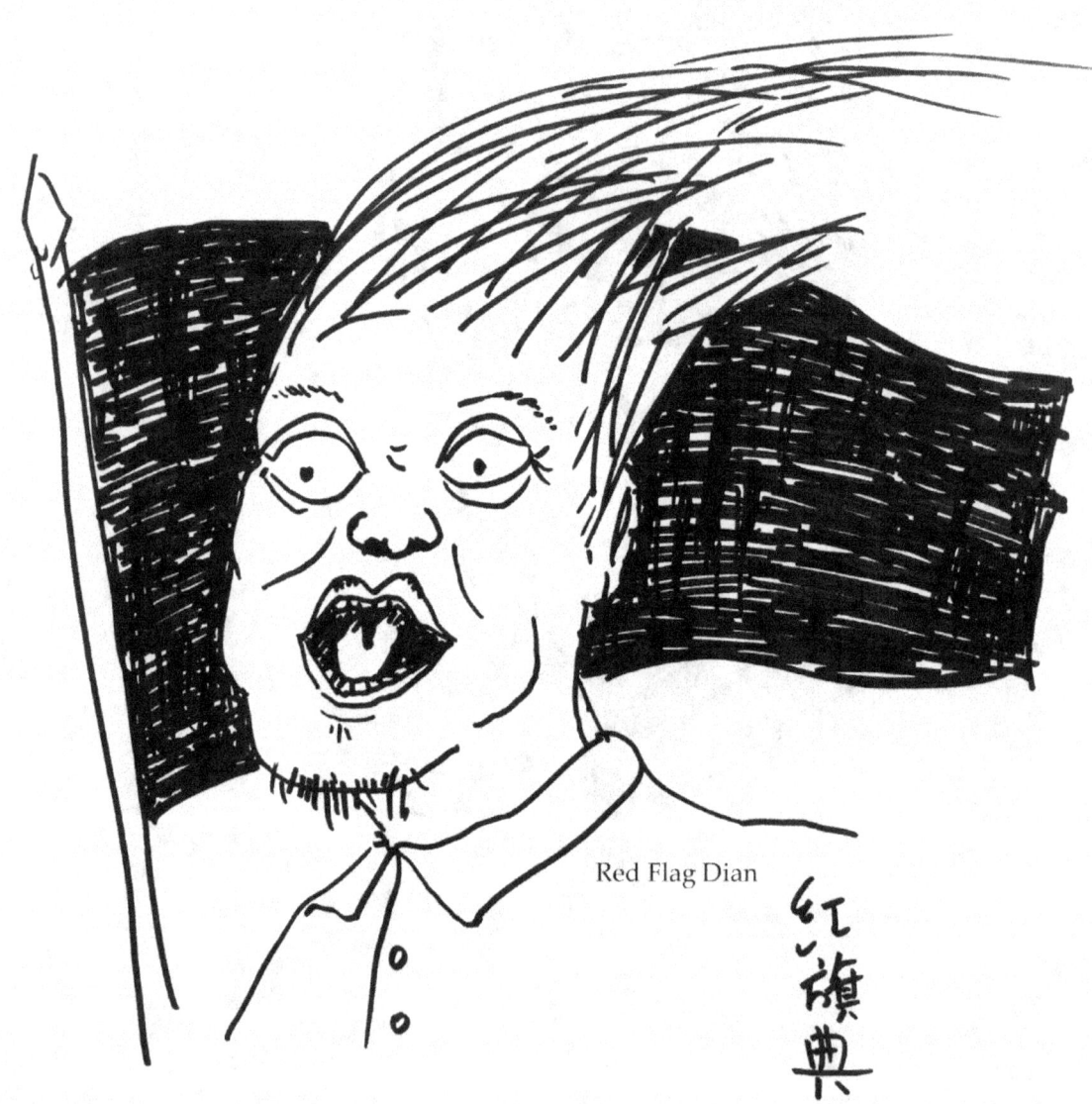

Red Flag Dian

红旗典

JONE
9-10-2015 金重

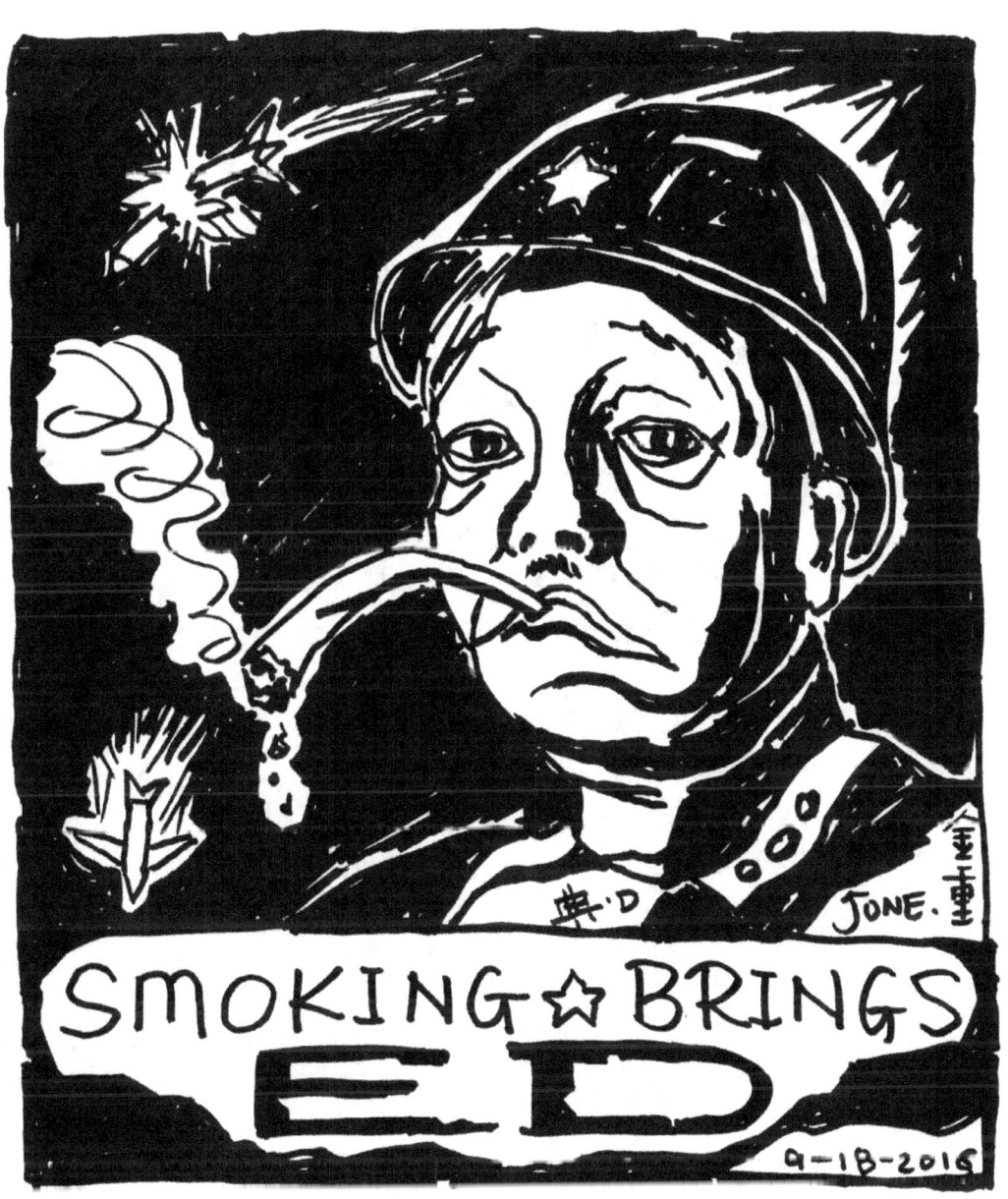

SMOKING ☆ BRINGS ED

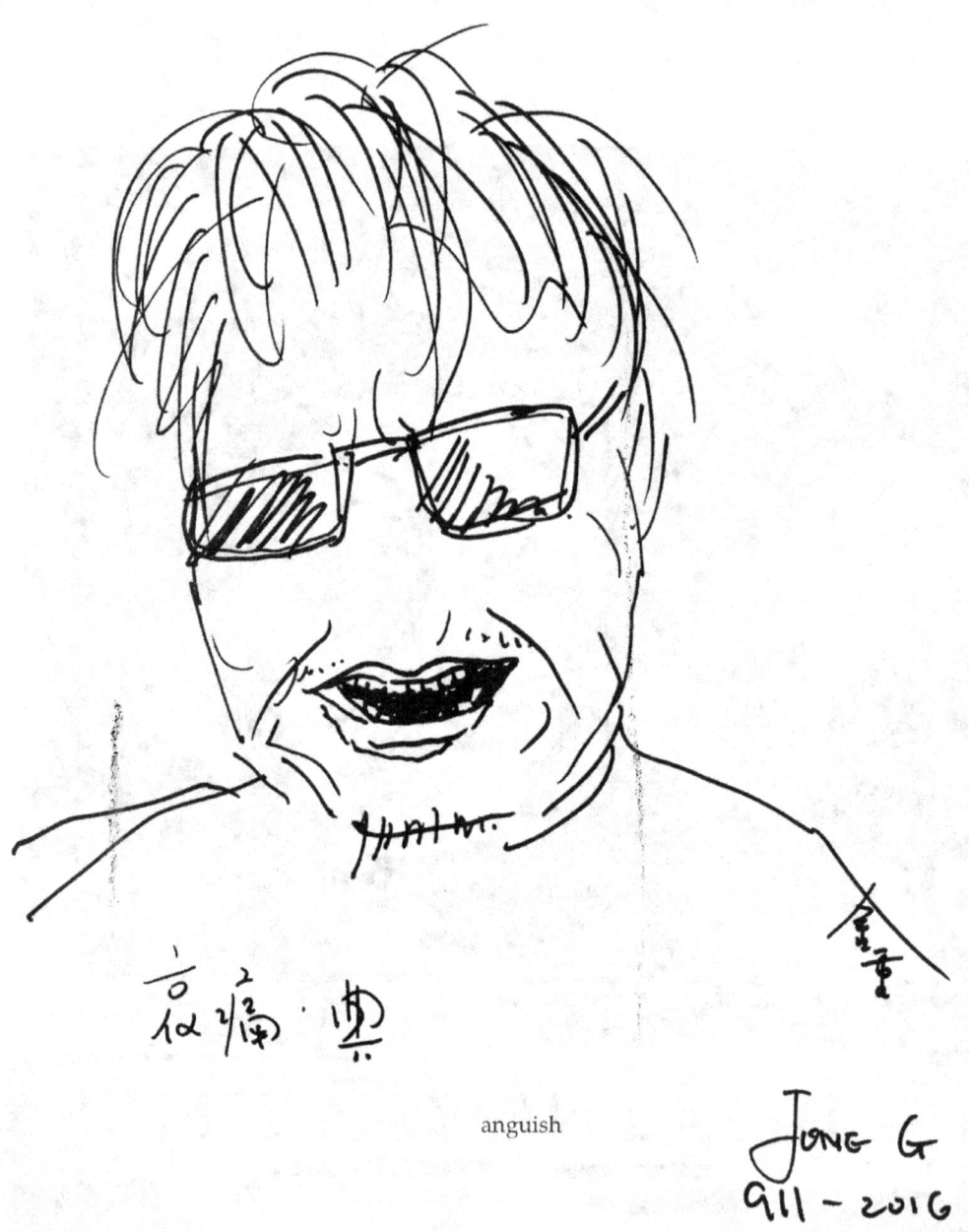

哀痛・樂

anguish

JONG G
911 - 2016

典裘沽酒的

故乡

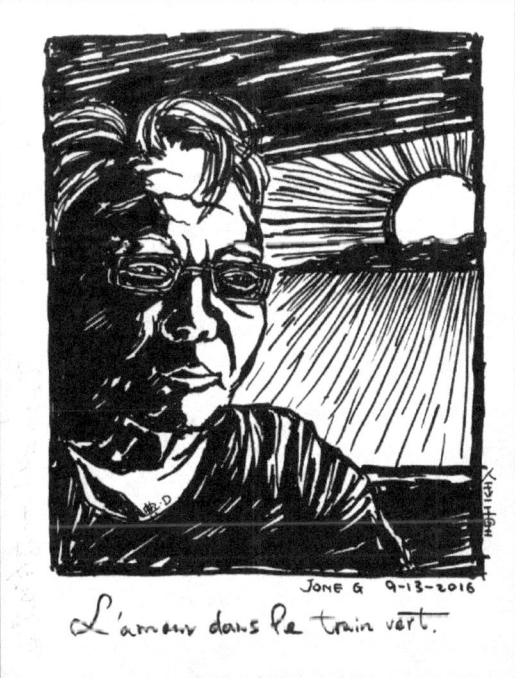

L'amour dans le train vert.

HOMETOWN

我恨你的忧郁
打开窗子
打开一百多个窗口的火车
湘江清澈无影
一排南归的鸿雁飞过

绿皮火车漂泊成白色
那候车的人，还在小站等

I am so afraid of your melancholy
Your opened window
Over one hundred opened windows
Of a train

The Xiang River
Shallow and shadowless
Some wild geese fly southbound
In a line

The green coat of the train
Fades in its endless travel
That passenger is still waiting
On this small town's platform

Dian Qiu
translated by Jin Zhong

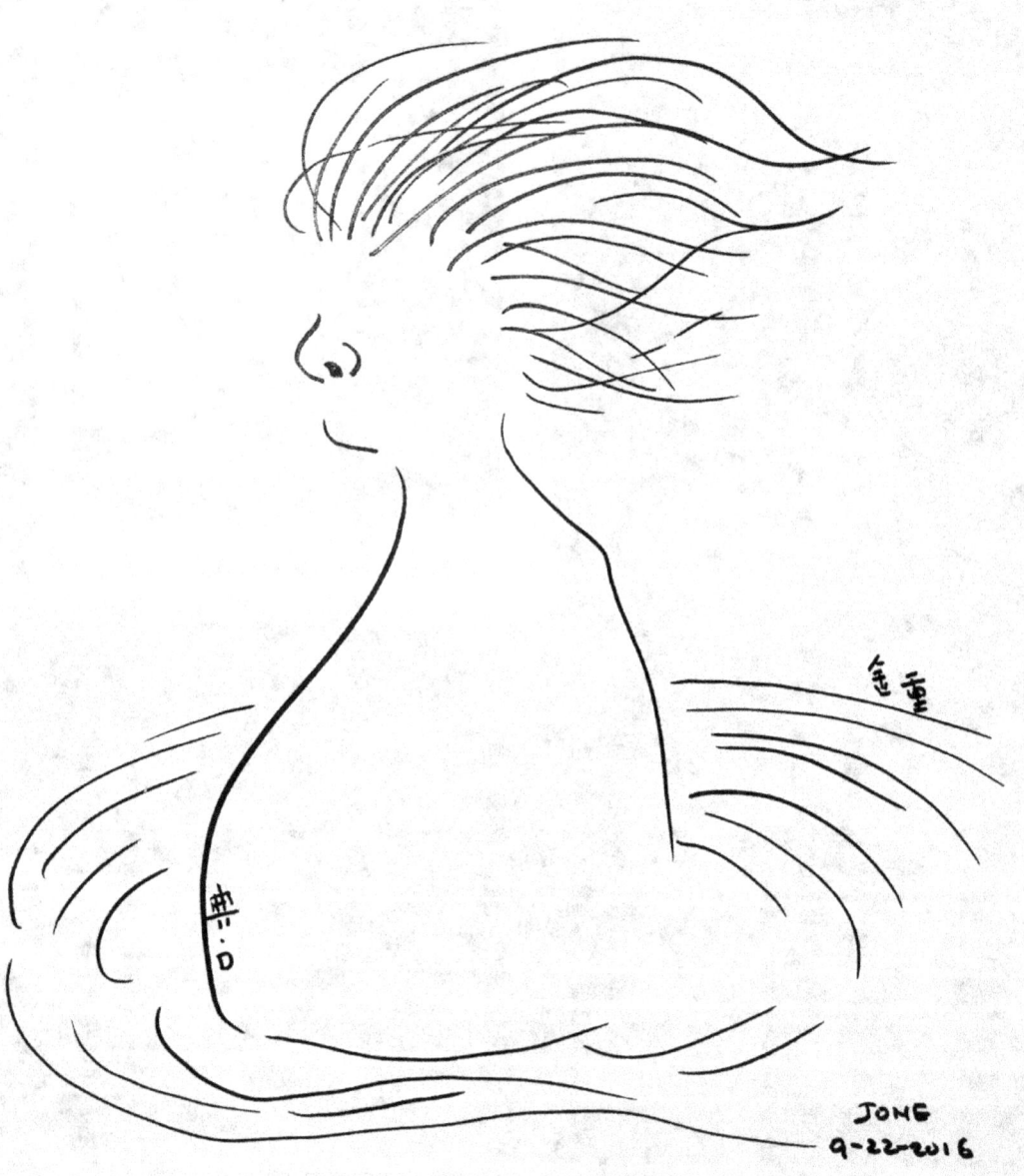

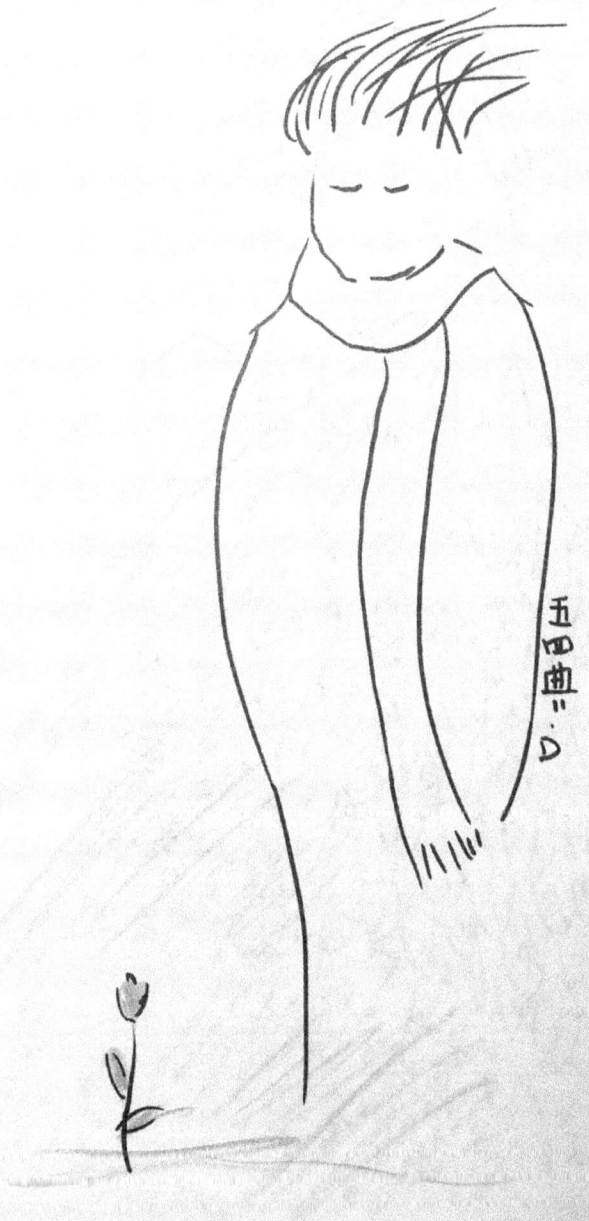

wild Dian

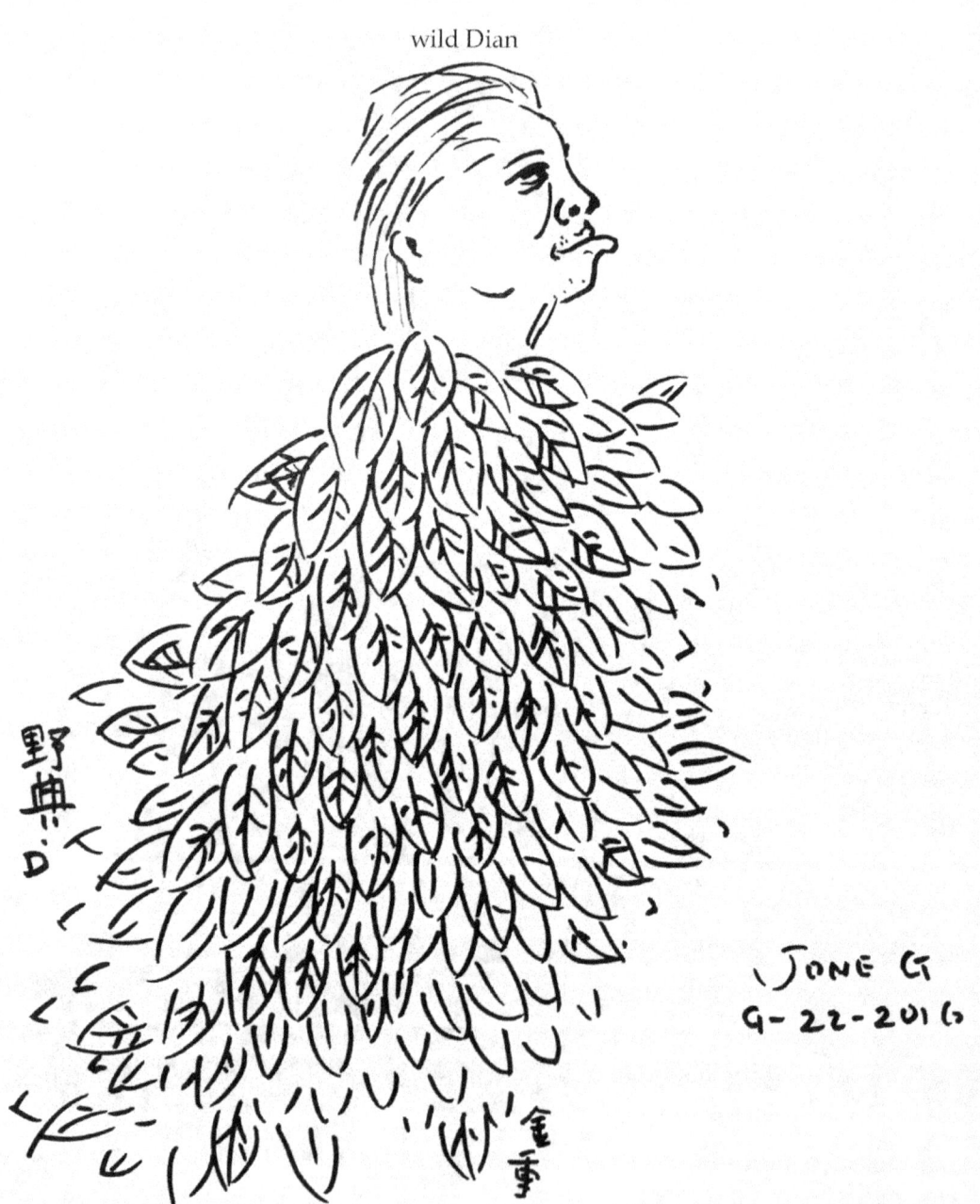

JONE G
6-22-2016

MY LIFE

一生

典裘

The beach. A pile of
Liquor bottles
Tonight all my drunken fellows
Are trapped inside
Sleepless thoughts drift in the wind
Reeds stand by the water
Aimlessly

I 've been a good man for my whole life
Yet infamous as a stinky fish

Dian Qiu
translated by Jin Zhong

海滩，一堆酒瓶
今夜，所有的酒友都关在里面
失眠在风中飞行
芦苇站在河边等

我一生善良
却臭名如死鱼

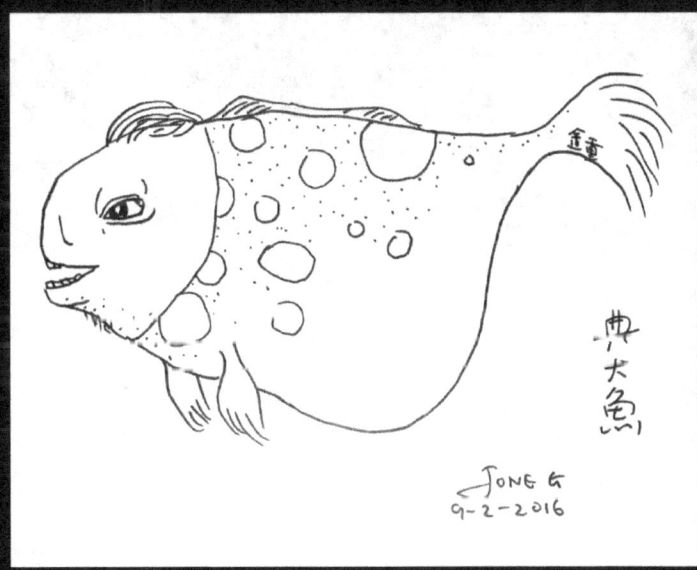

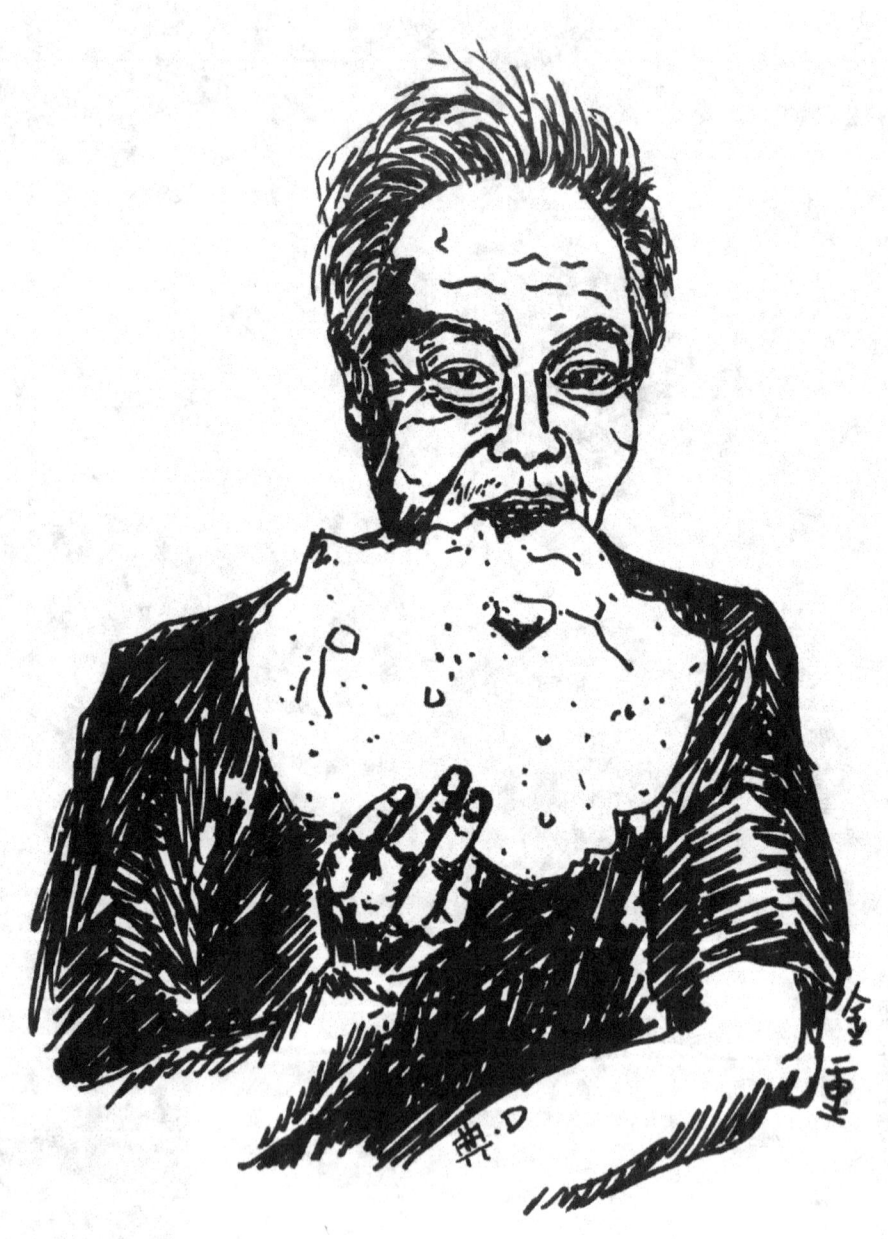

Draw Dian Qiu if hungry

JUNE G
10-15-2016

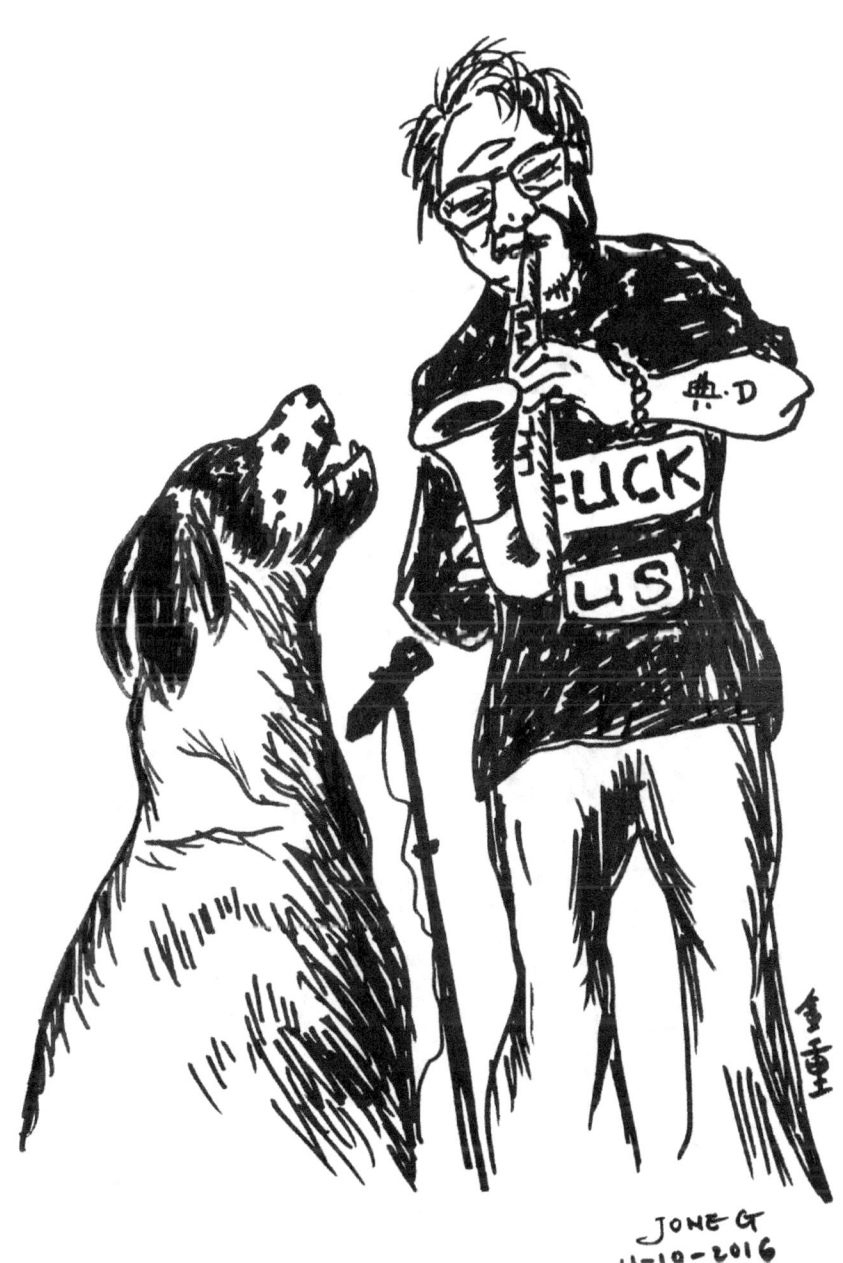

JONE G
11-10-2016

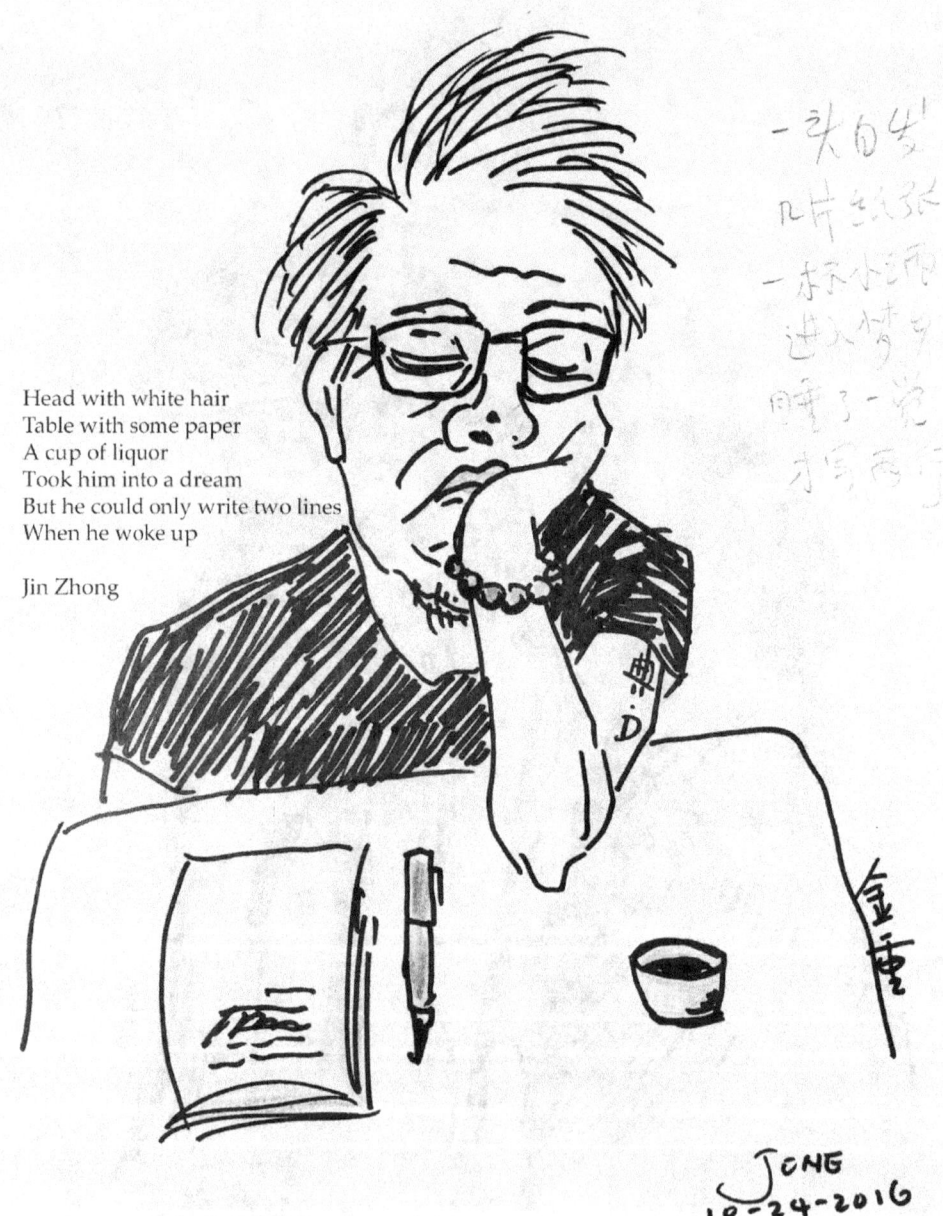

Head with white hair
Table with some paper
A cup of liquor
Took him into a dream
But he could only write two lines
When he woke up

Jin Zhong

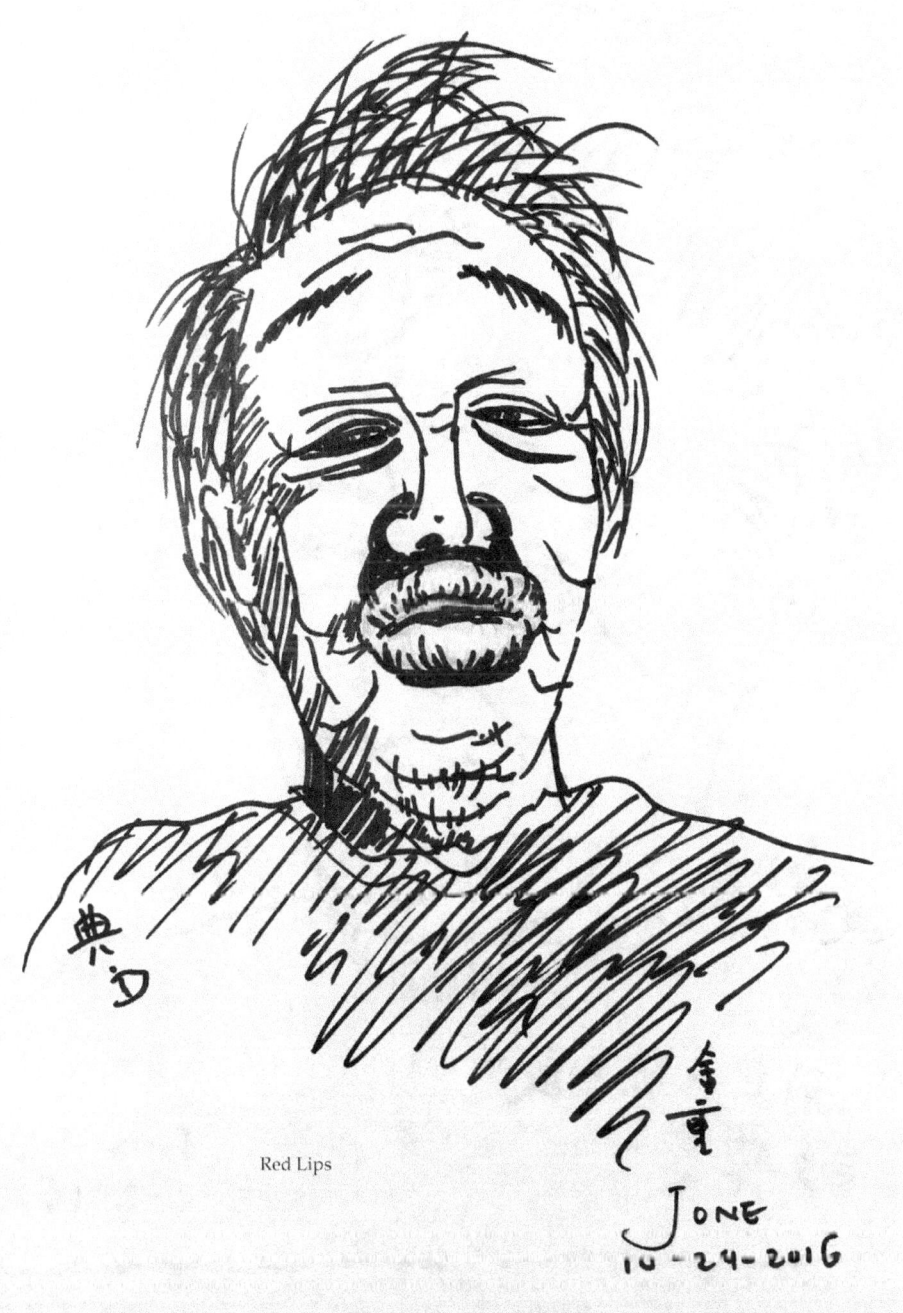

Red Lips

JONE
10-24-2016

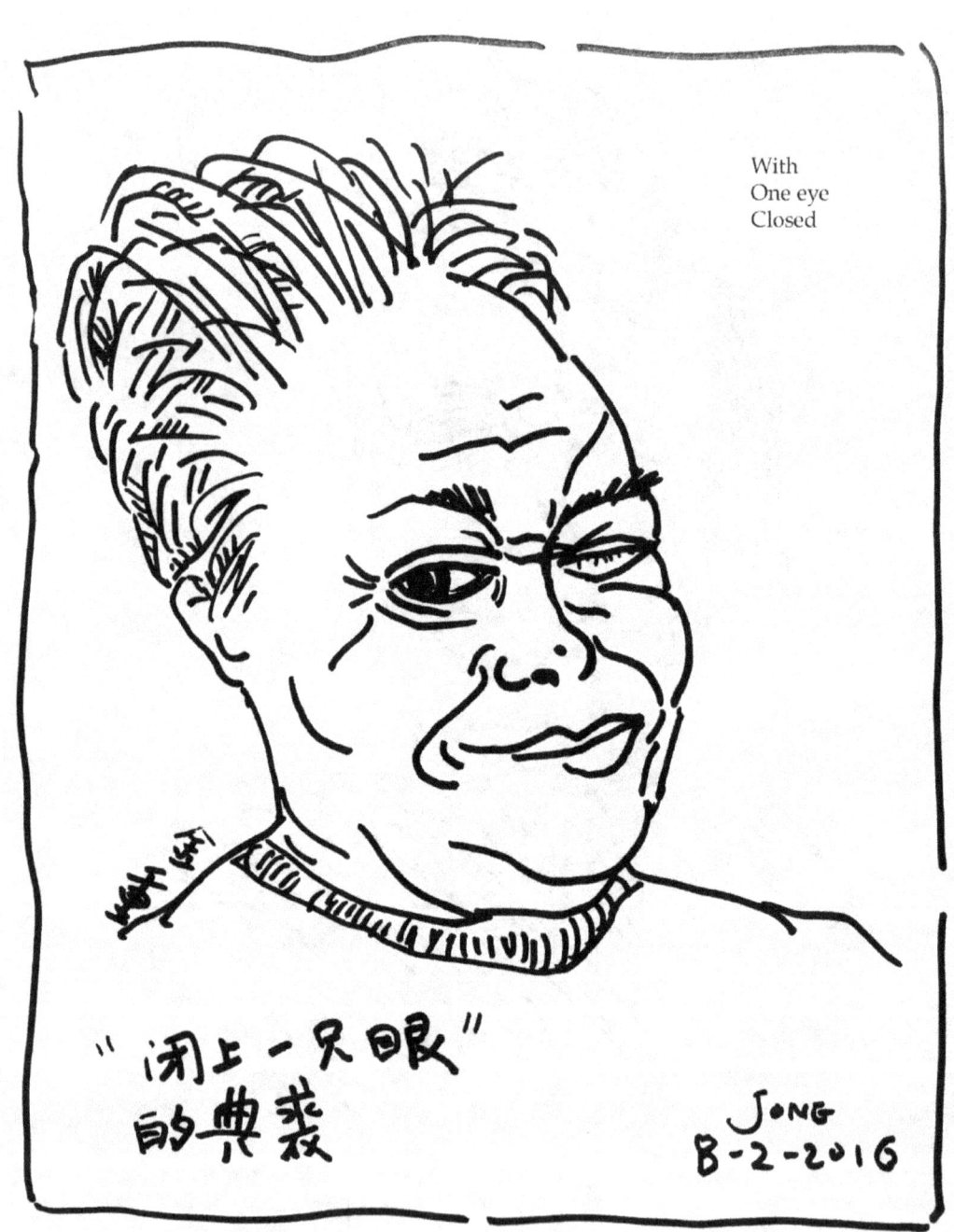

With
One eye
Closed

"闭上一只眼"
的典裁

JONG
8-2-2016

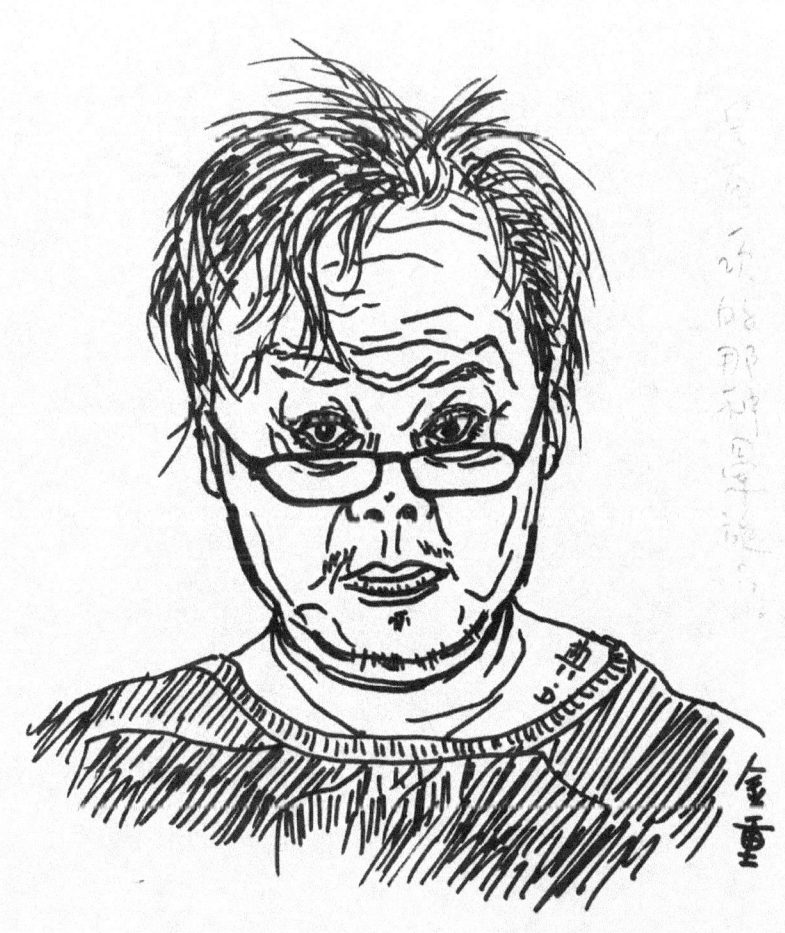

11-22-2016

JUNE

That dizziness
I just experienced
Once

--Dian Qiu

Dian Dian Dian Dian...
Beijing Beijing Beijing ...

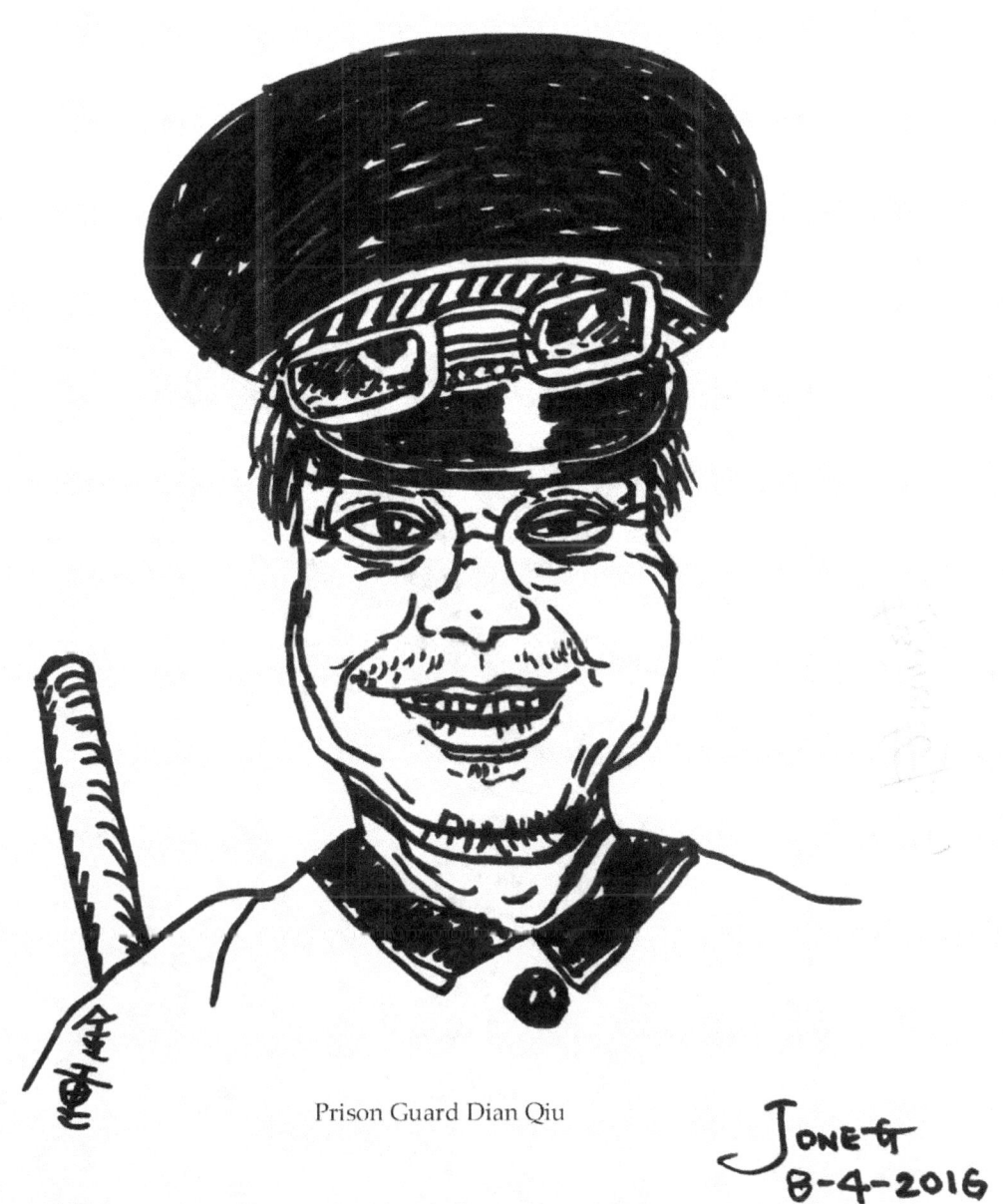

Prison Guard Dian Qiu

JONE G
8-4-2016

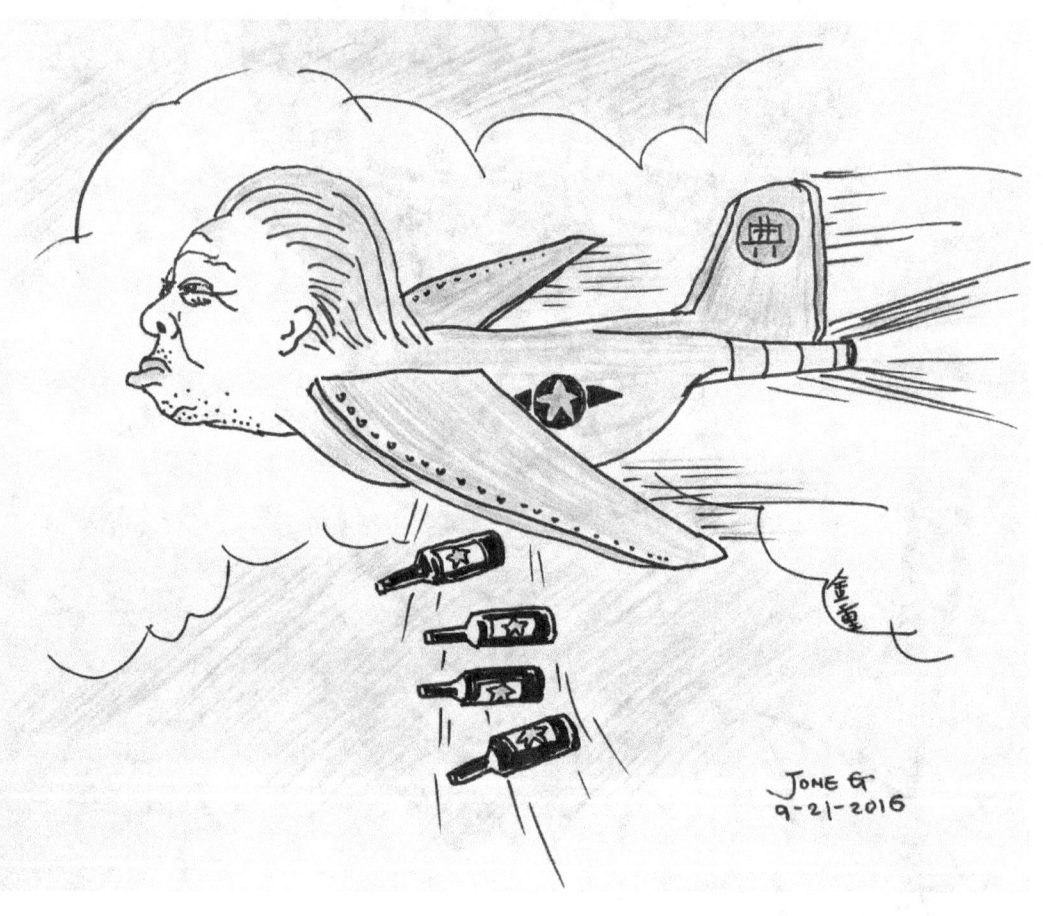

JONE G
9-21-2016

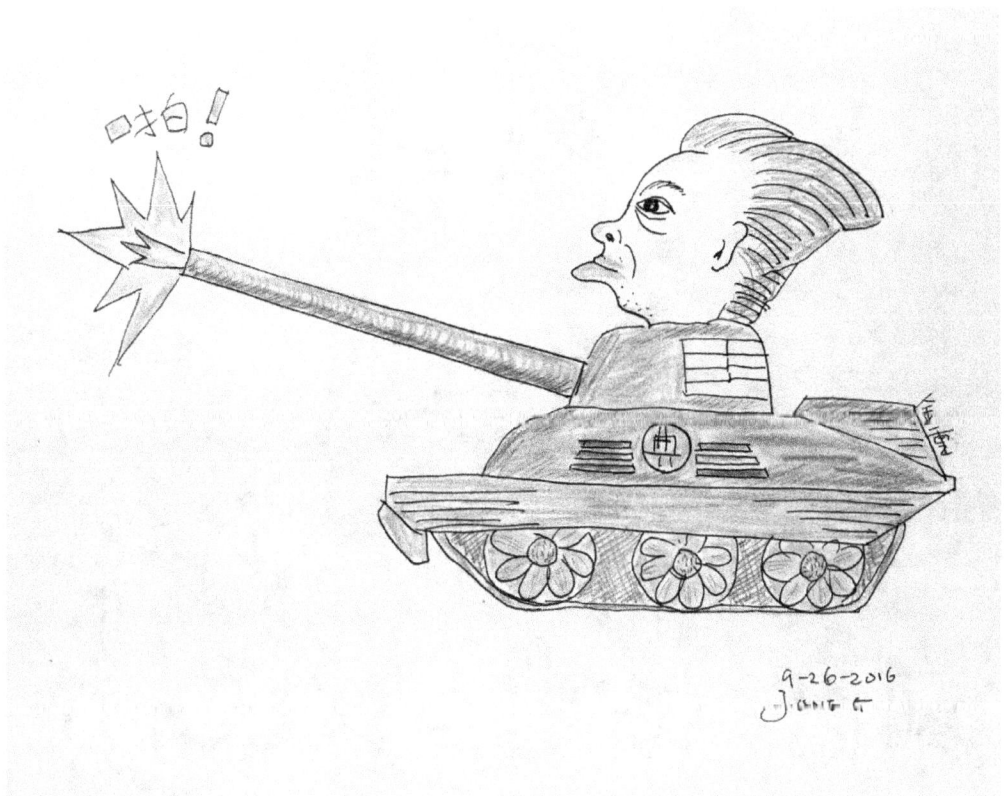

Third hour
After Noble Prize is announced...

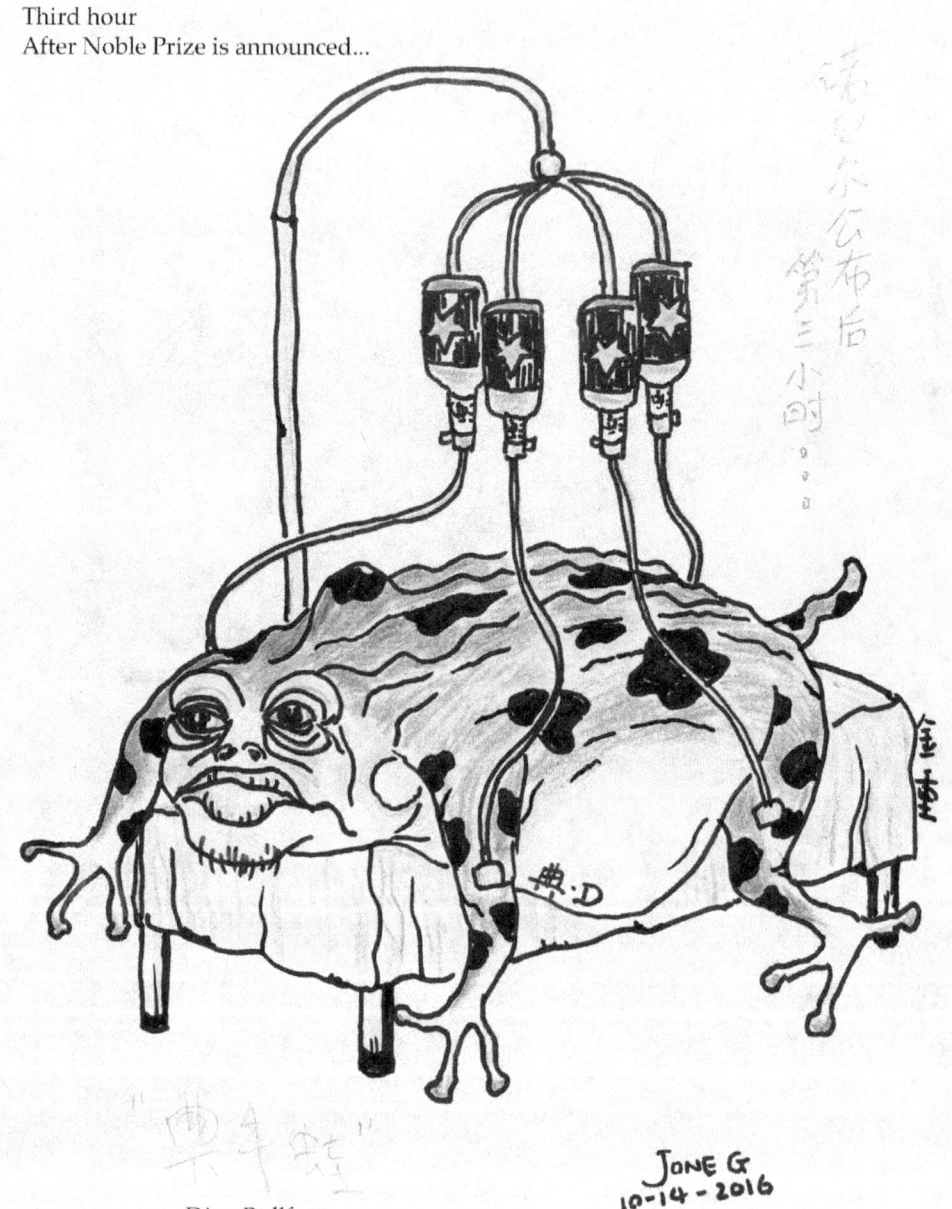

Dian Bullfrog

JONE G
10-14-2016

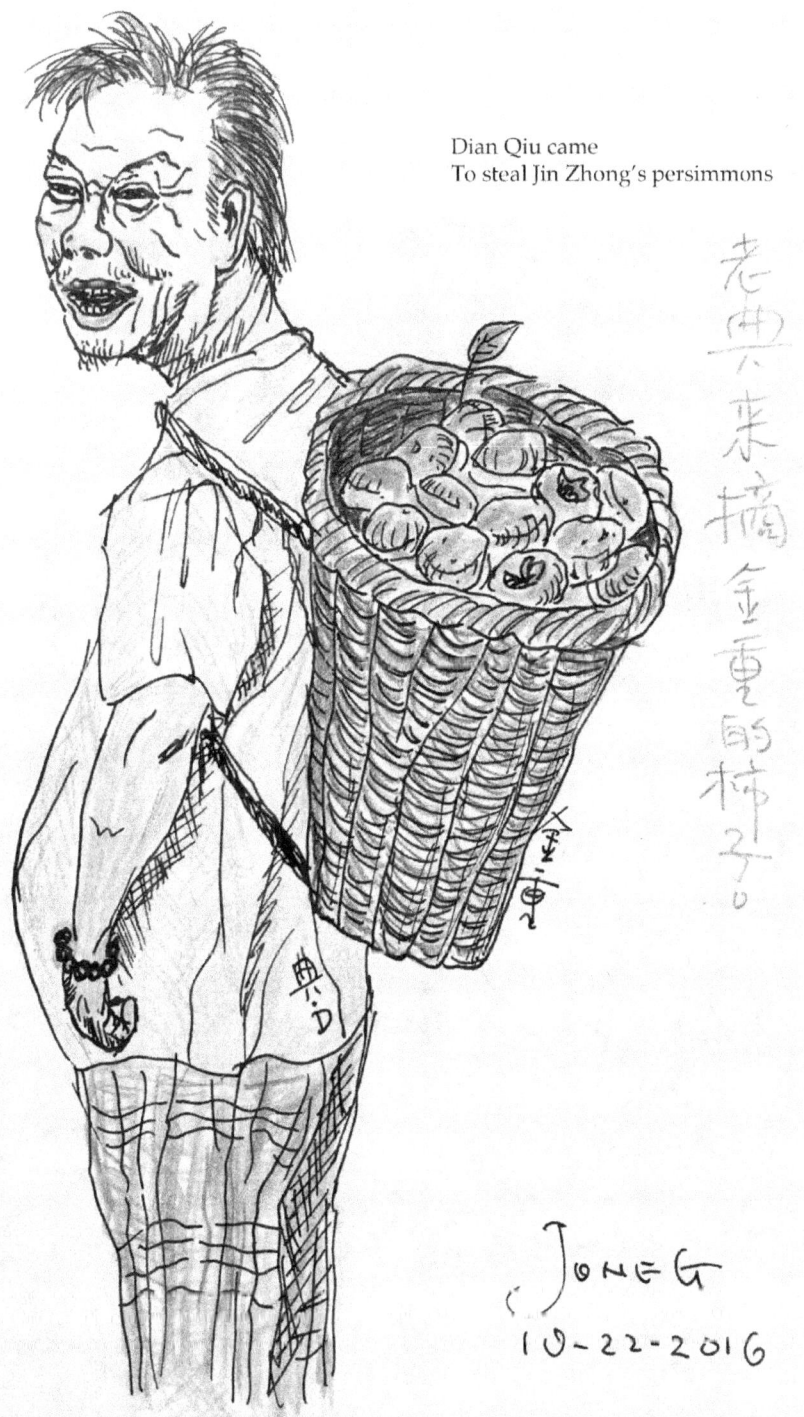

Dian Qiu came
To steal Jin Zhong's persimmons

老典来摘金重的柿子。

JONEG
10-22-2016

47

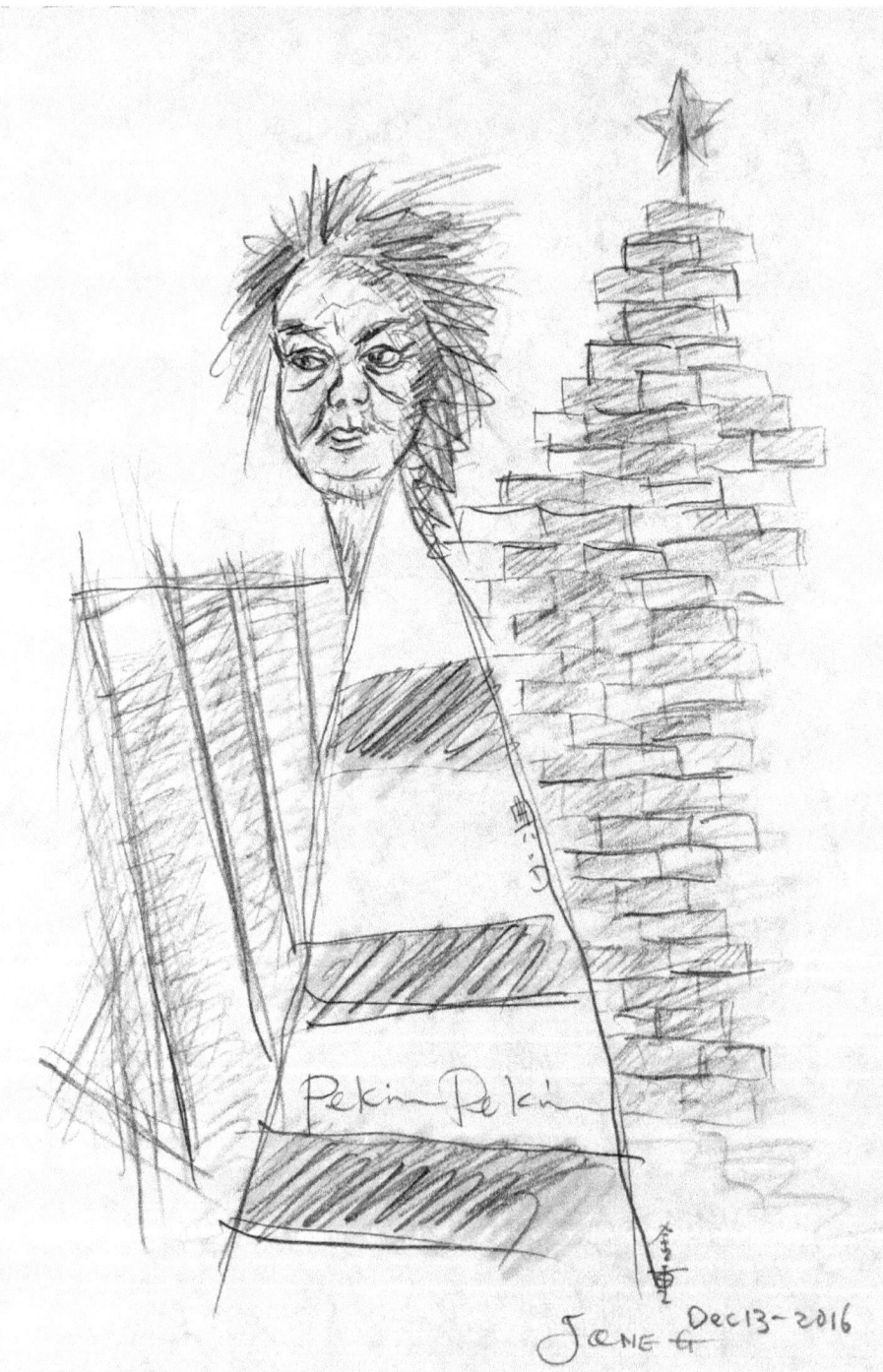

Pekin Pekin

Janet Dec13-2016

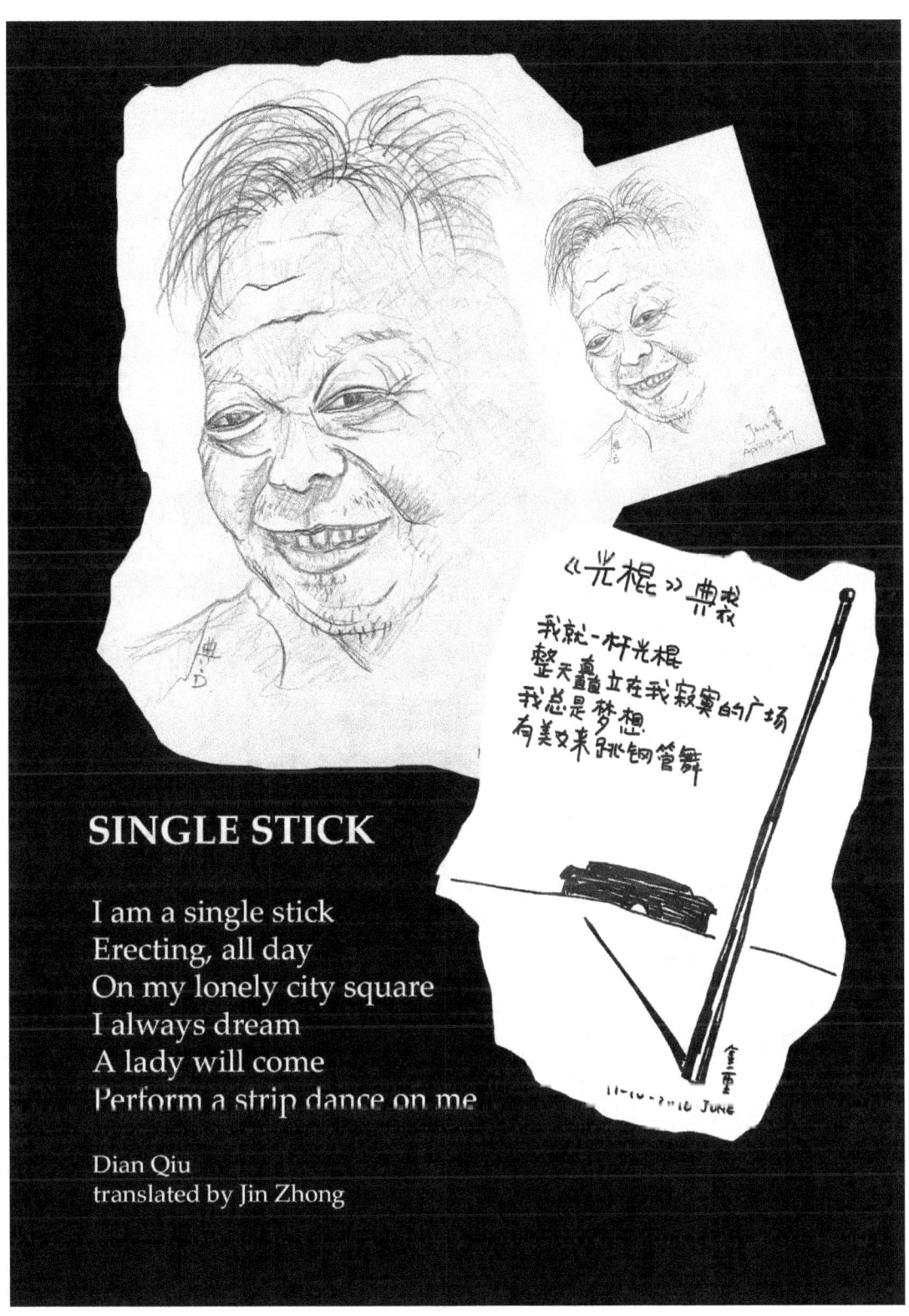

SINGLE STICK

I am a single stick
Erecting, all day
On my lonely city square
I always dream
A lady will come
Perform a strip dance on me

Dian Qiu
translated by Jin Zhong

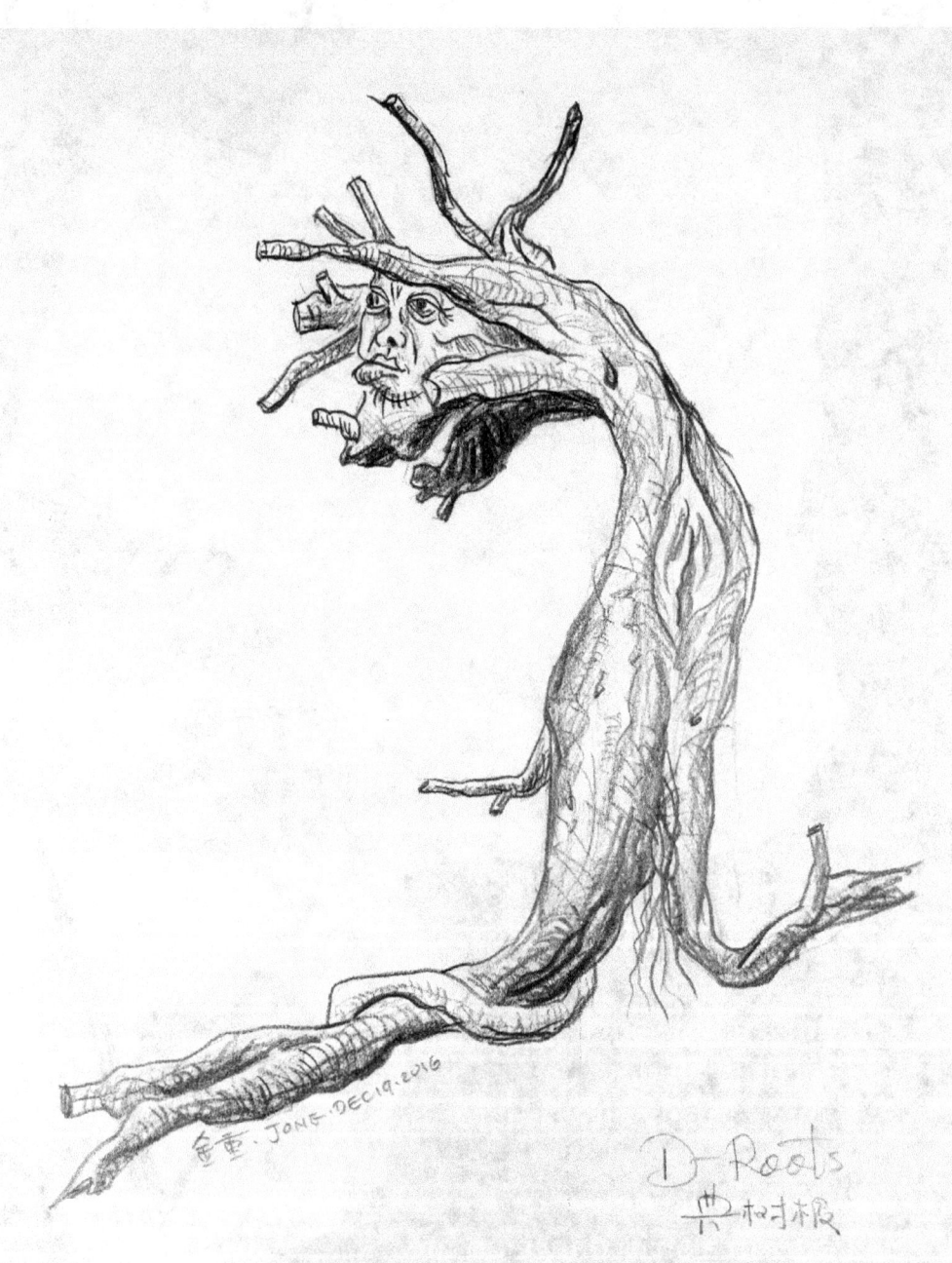

鐘重. JONE. DEC.19.2016

D. Roots
典相村根

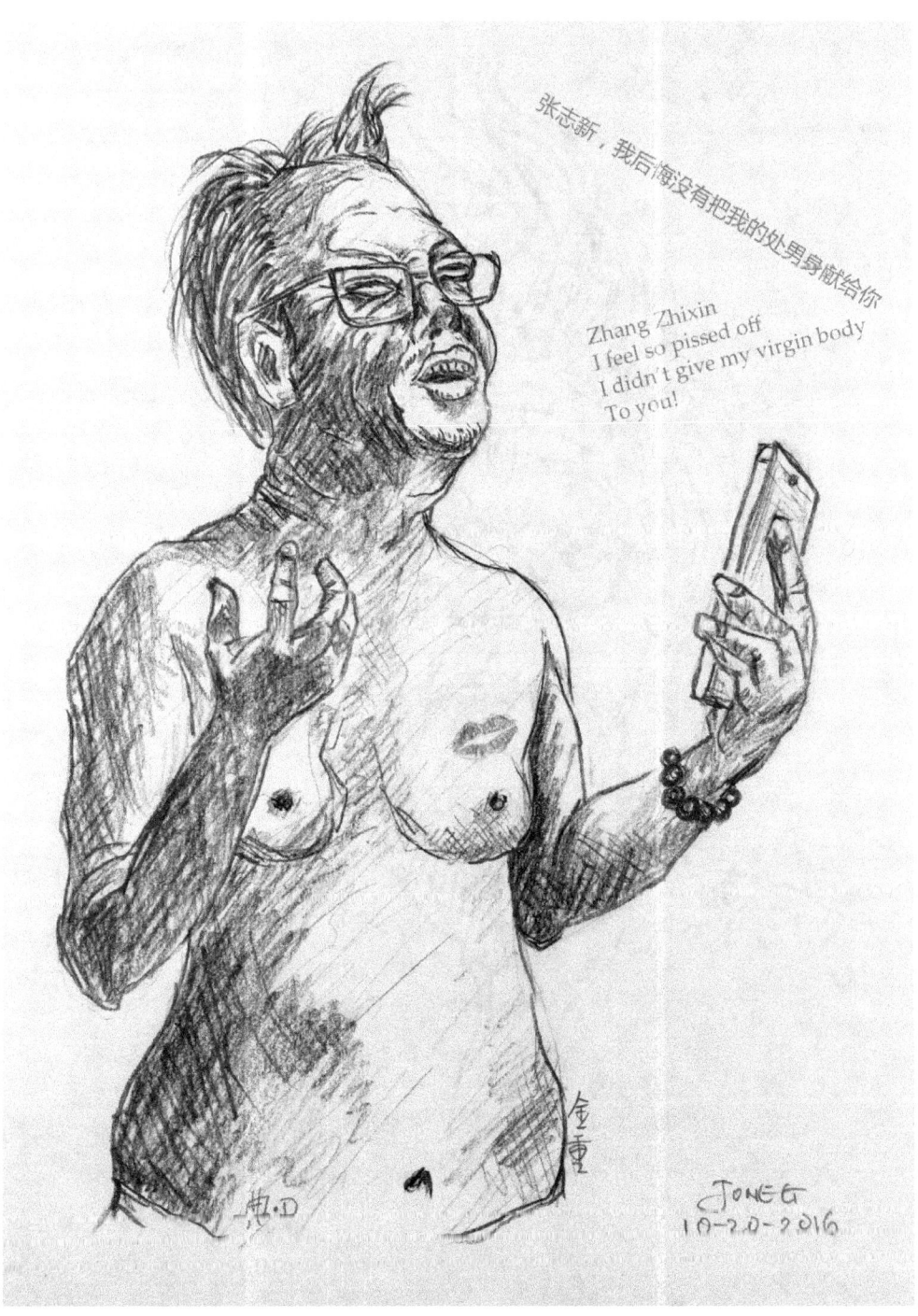

Who is Zhang?   https://en.wikipedia.org/wiki/Zhang_Zhixin

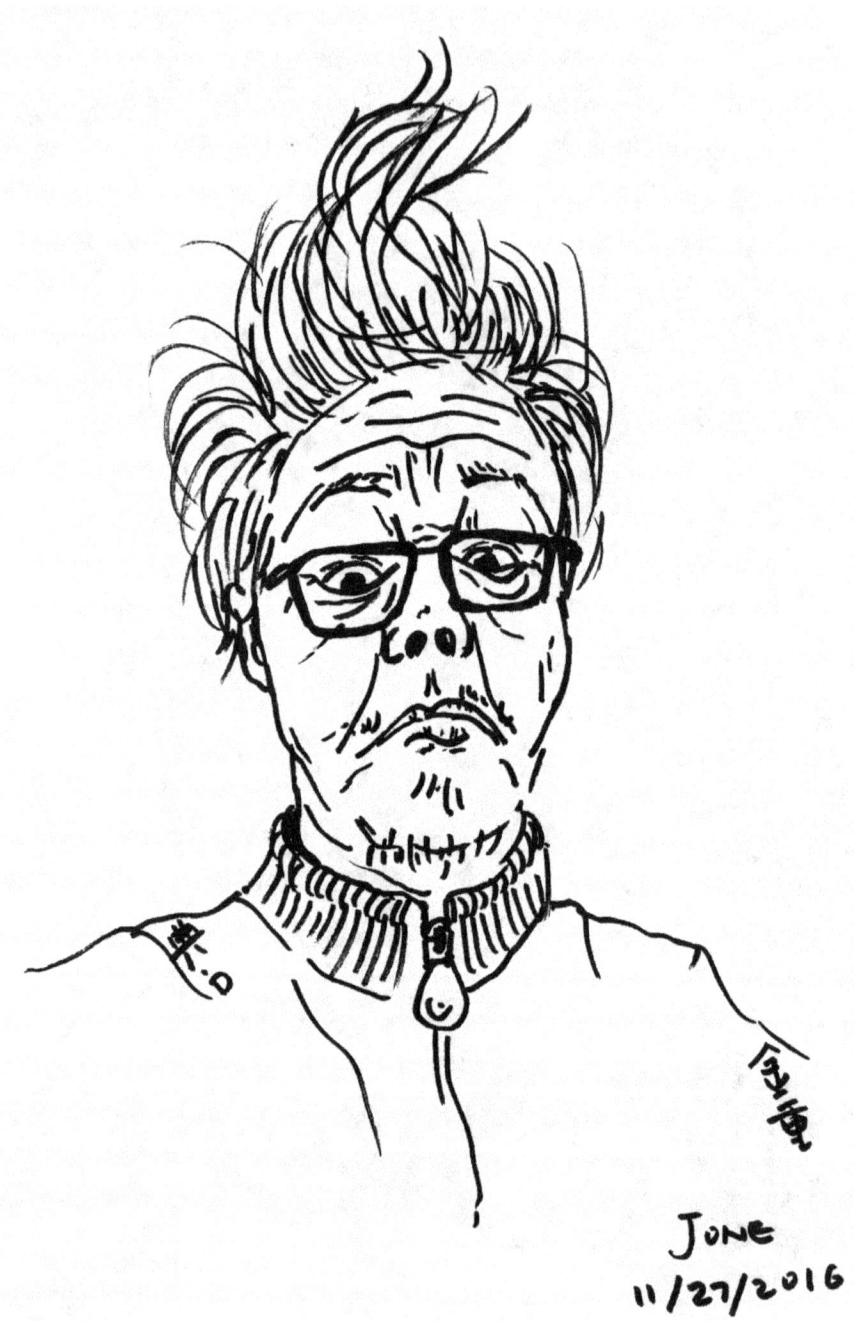

JUNE
11/27/2016

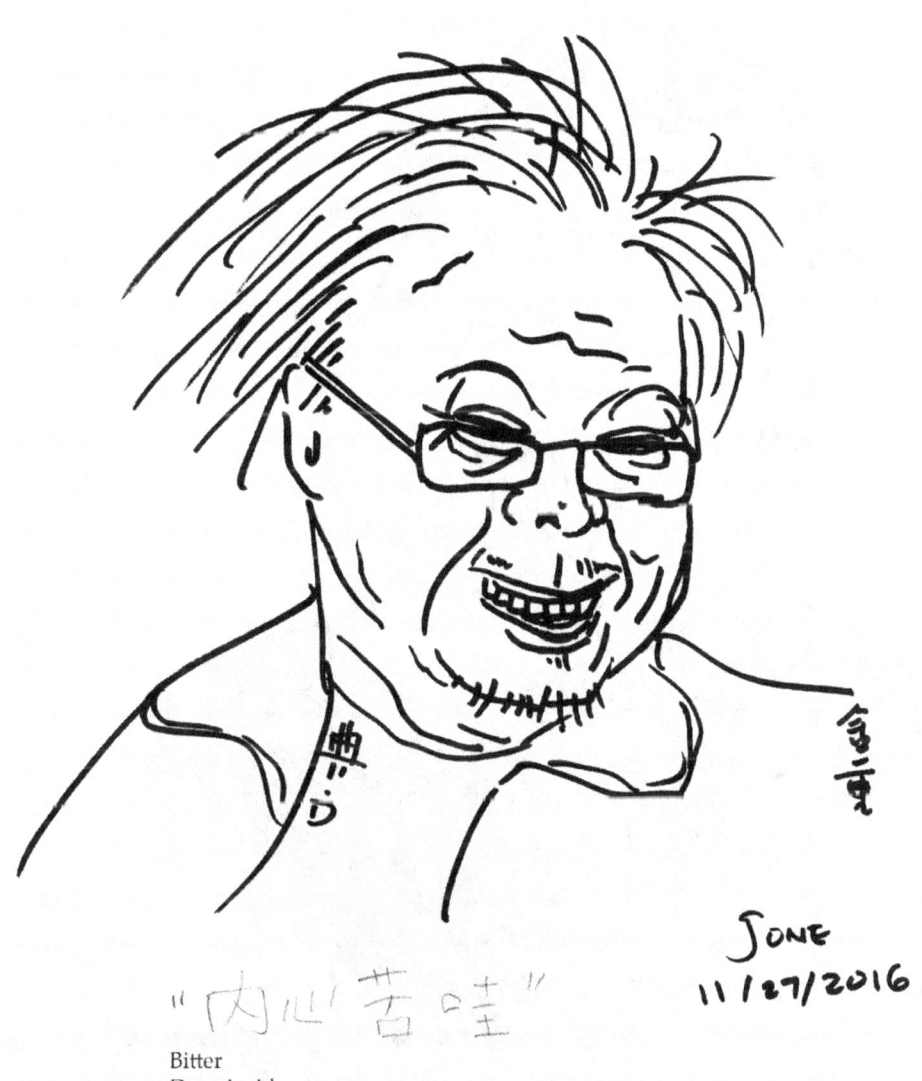

"内心苦哇"

Bitter
Deep inside

Jone
11/27/2016

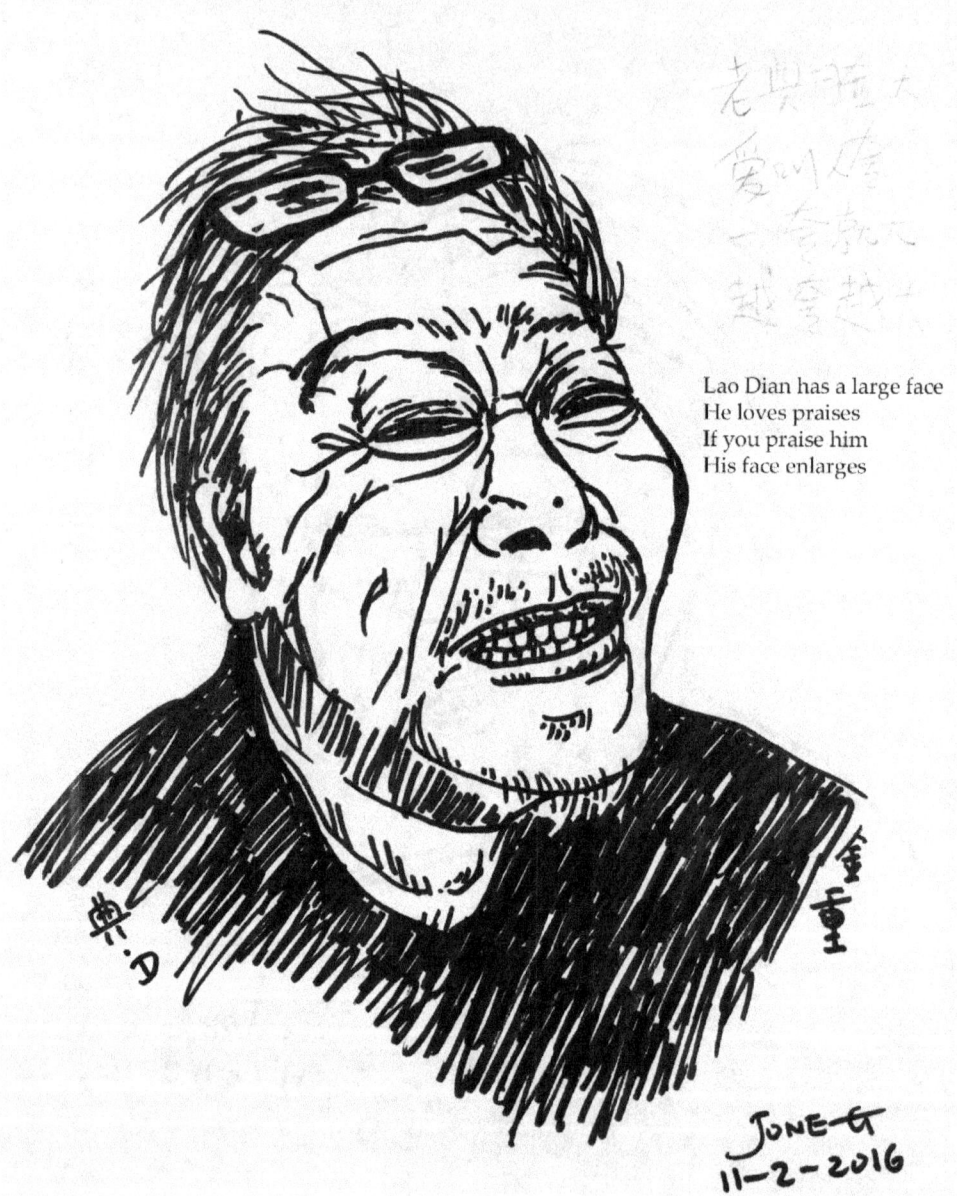

老點臉大
愛叫唯
一叫就大
越吹越大

Lao Dian has a large face
He loves praises
If you praise him
His face enlarges

JUNE-G
11-2-2016

Freedom

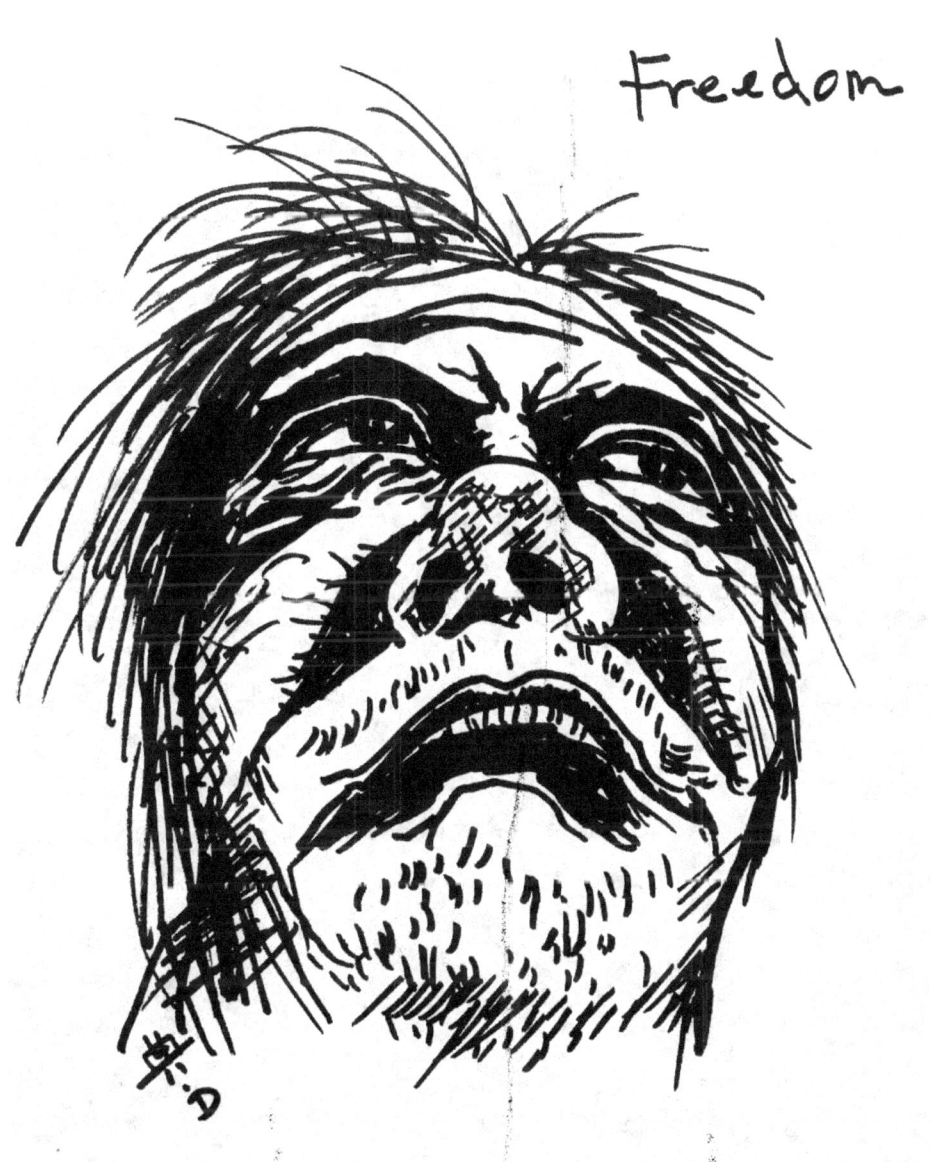

JONE 金
5/21/2017 鐘

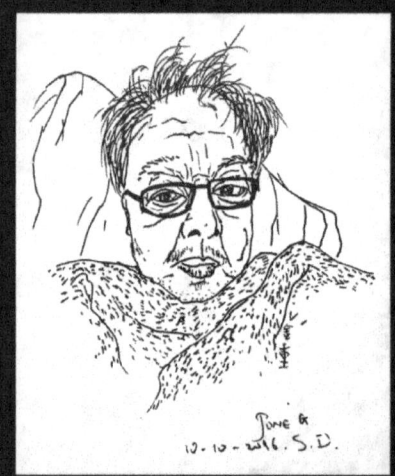

写给外国的富婆们　典裘

亲，我实在是活不下了
在我的祖国
大米、水、肉、油和奶都有毒
叫我肿么活下去

亲，请收留我吧
就当收留一只流浪狗
我宁愿去舔
开在山谷里寂寞的
黑木耳
也不想
在这片总是让我饱含泪水的土地上
继续做中国梦
做宪政梦

20B年5月25日广州

FOR RICH LADIES OVERSEAS

Honey, listen, I am dying
In my own country
Rice, water, pork, cooking oil and milk
All contaminated
Tell me, how can I survive all these?
Honey, bring me home
Like adopting a dog from the shelter
I'd rather go and lick
Those lonesome black-eared fungi
Blooming in your valley
Than go on with
My Chinese Dream
My Dream of Constitutionalism
On this teary land
This land I was born and raised

May25, 2013
Dian Qiu
translated by Jin Zhong

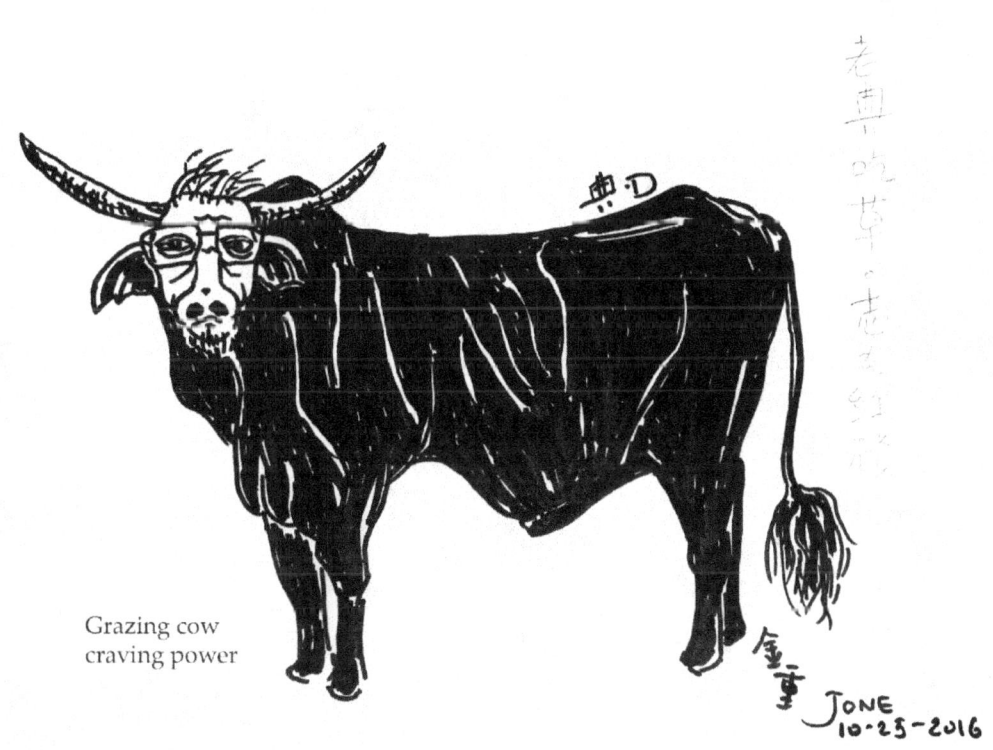

Grazing cow
craving power

老牛吃草，志在千里

金重 Jone
10-25-2016

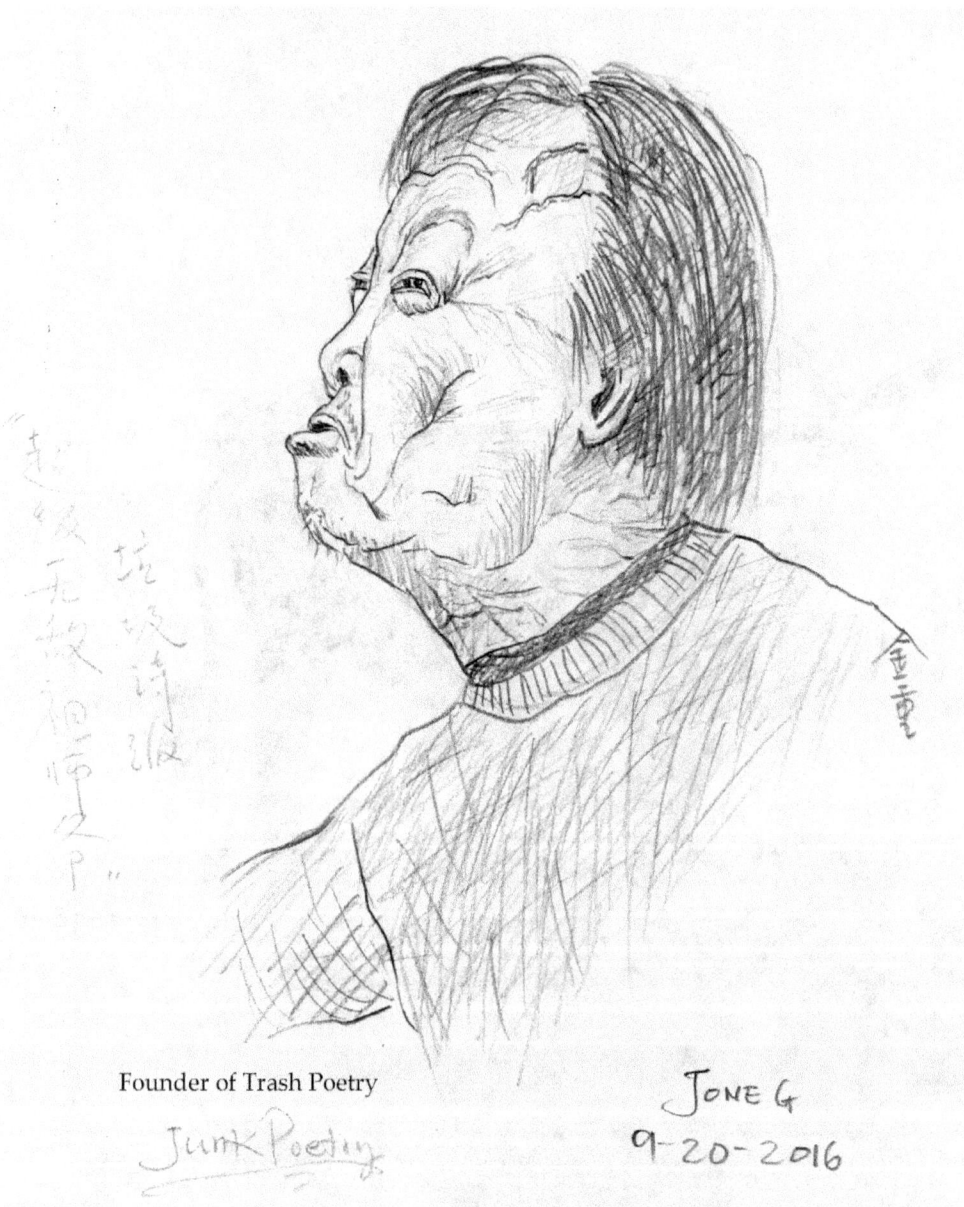

垃圾诗派

"先锋无效相声又P"

Founder of Trash Poetry

Junk Poetry

JONE G
9-20-2016

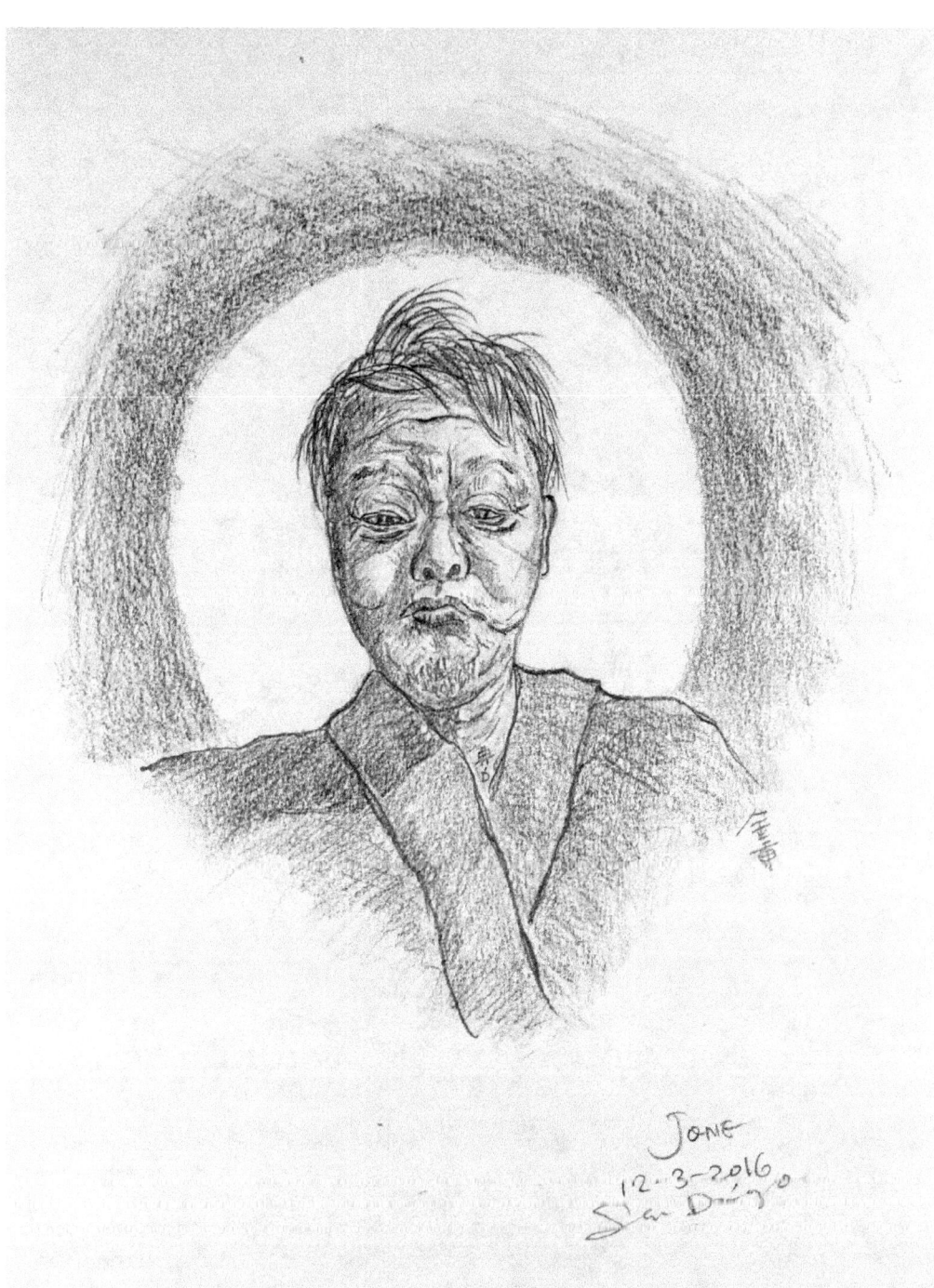

JONE
12.3.2016
San Diego.

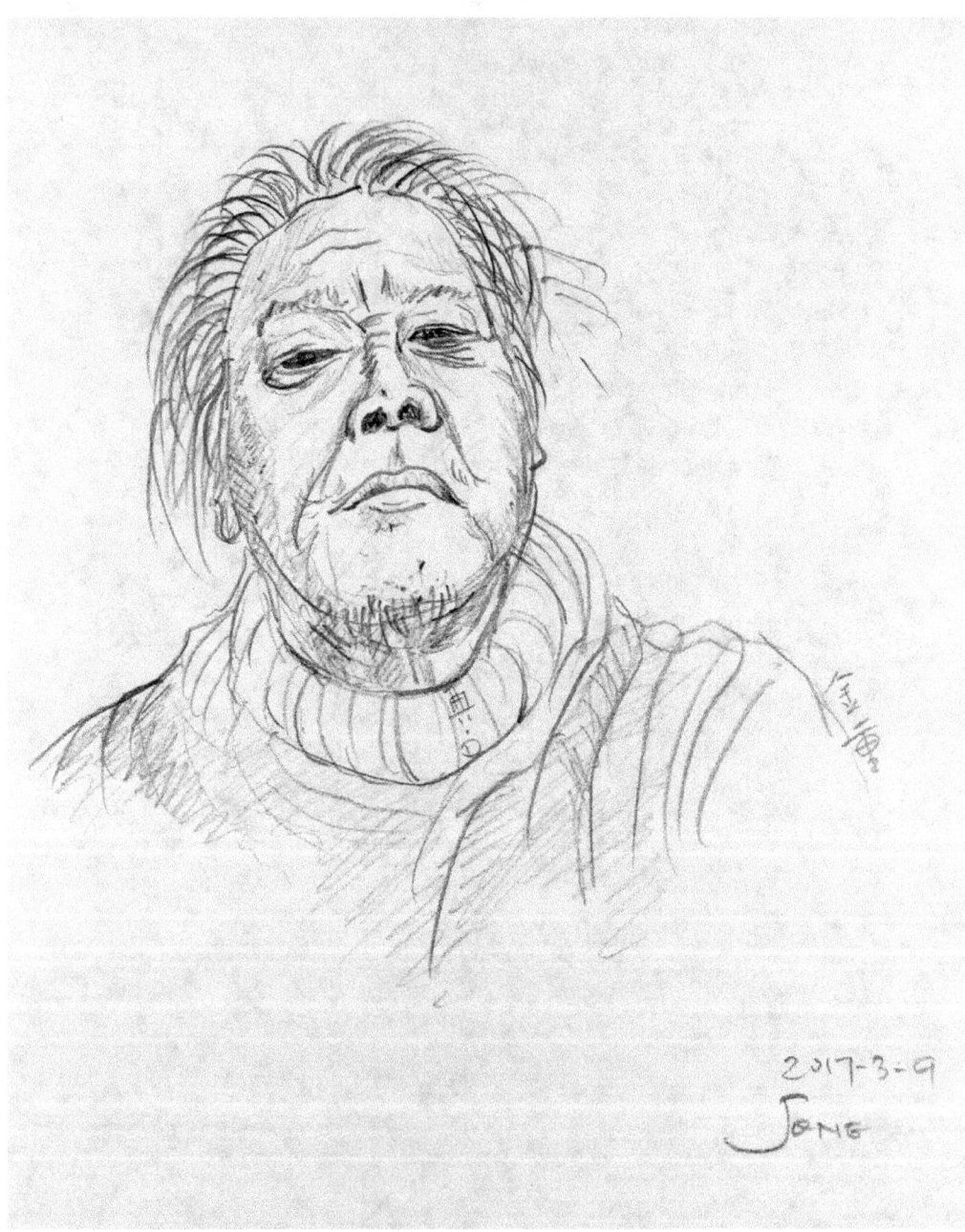

2017-3-9
JONG

上海法官日妓 典裘

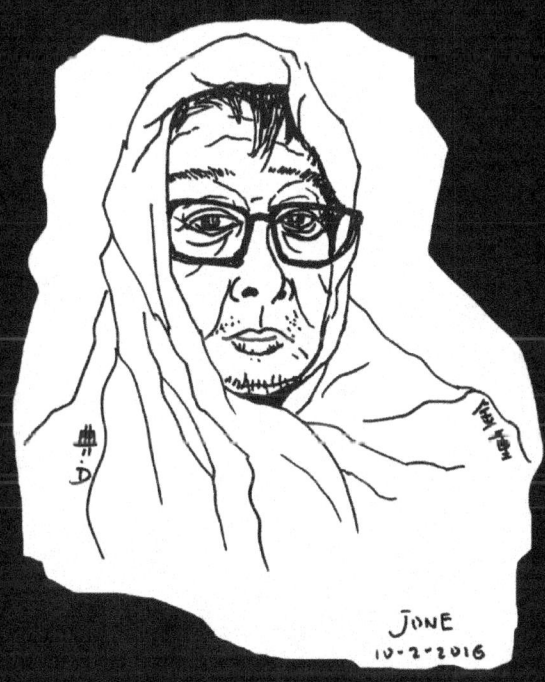

今天
我用锤子
敲了一下她的阴户
叫了一声
肃静

跟着
又敲了一下
又叫了一声
开庭

SHANGHAI JUDGE'S BROTHEL DIARY

Today
I pick up my gavel
And hit her vagina
Shouting:
Silence

I hit her again
I shout again:
This court is now in session

Dian Qiu
Translated by Jin Zhong

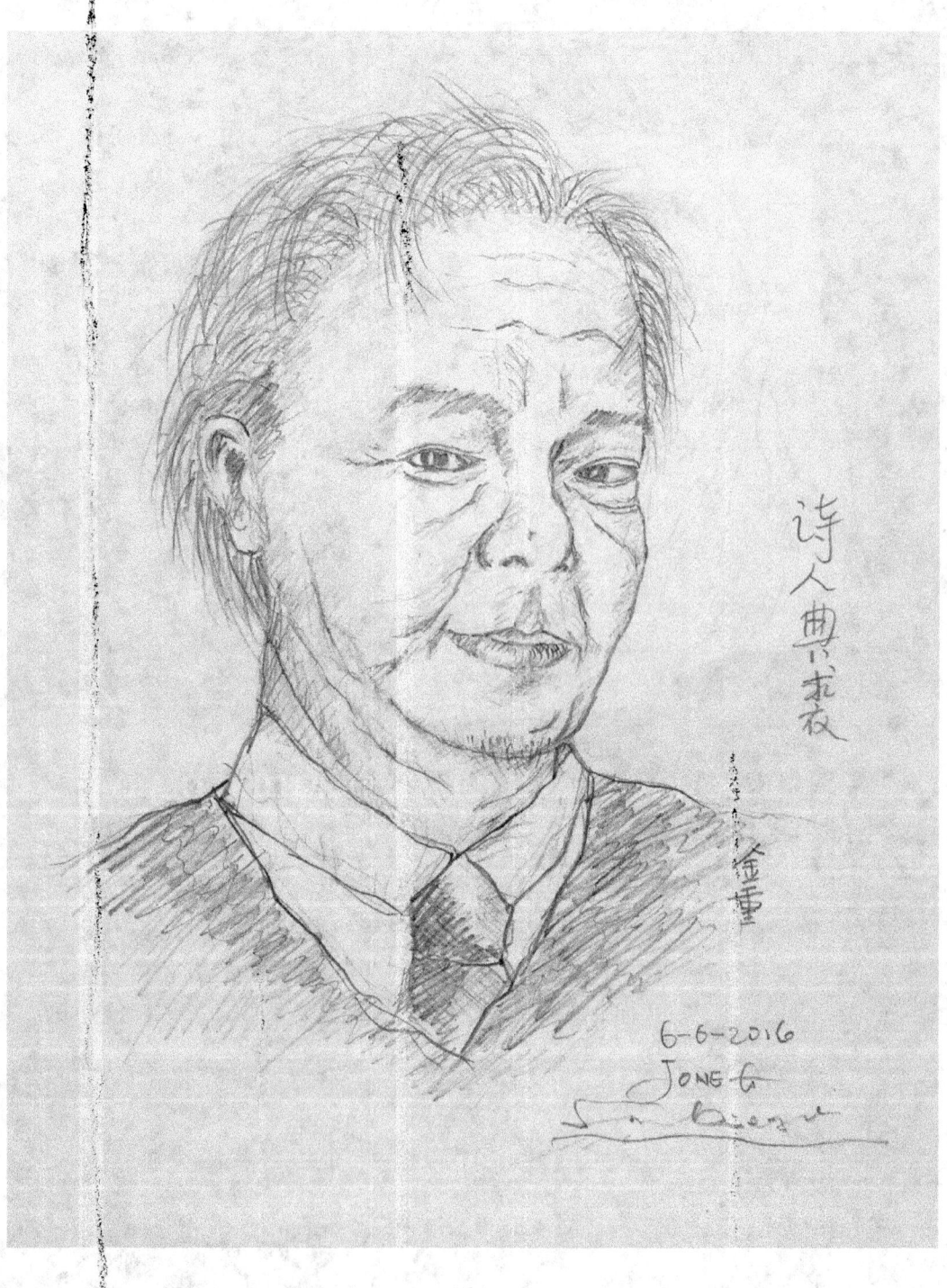

诗人典求夜

金重

6-6-2016
JONE G

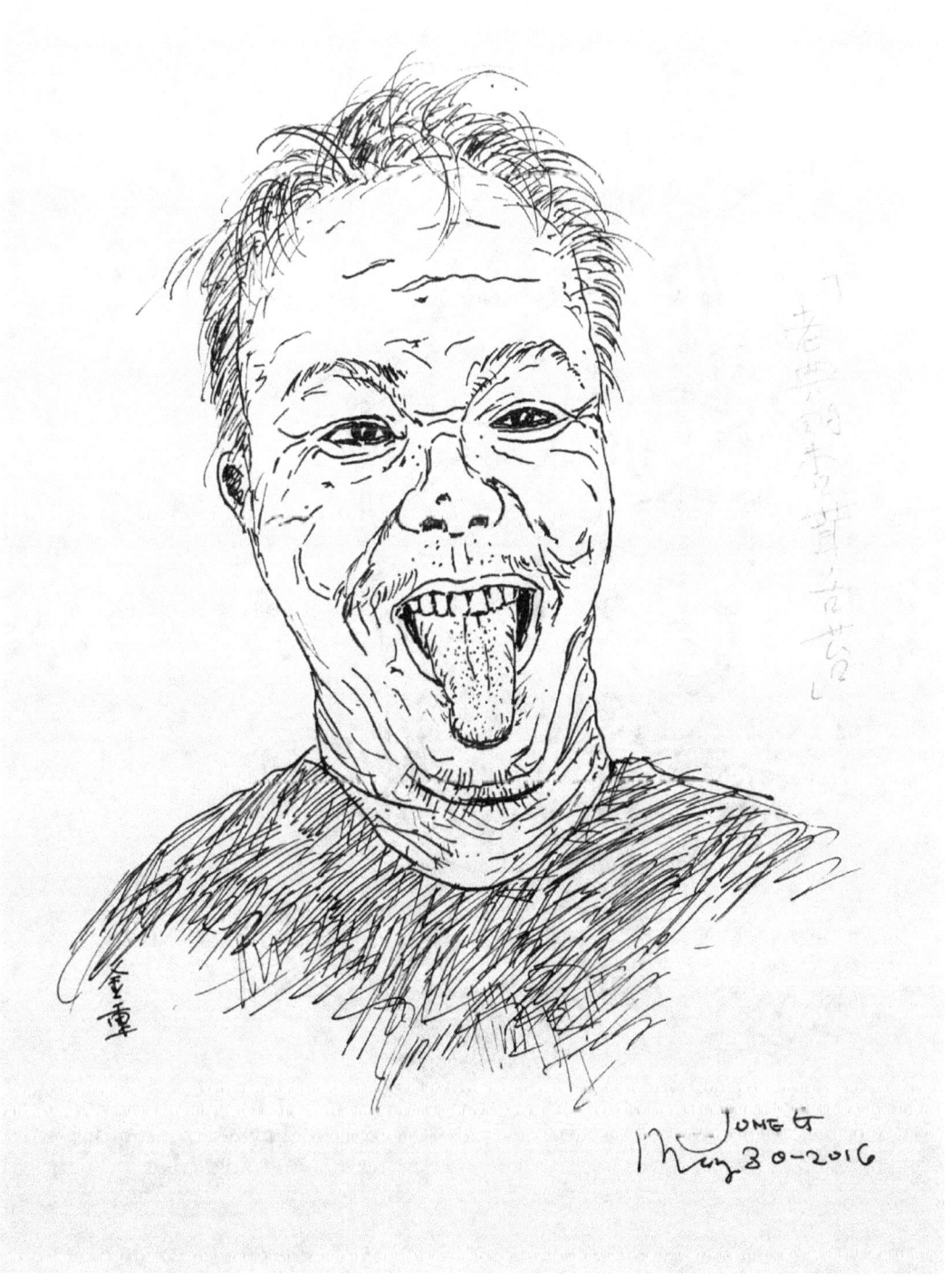

JUNE 4
May 30-2016

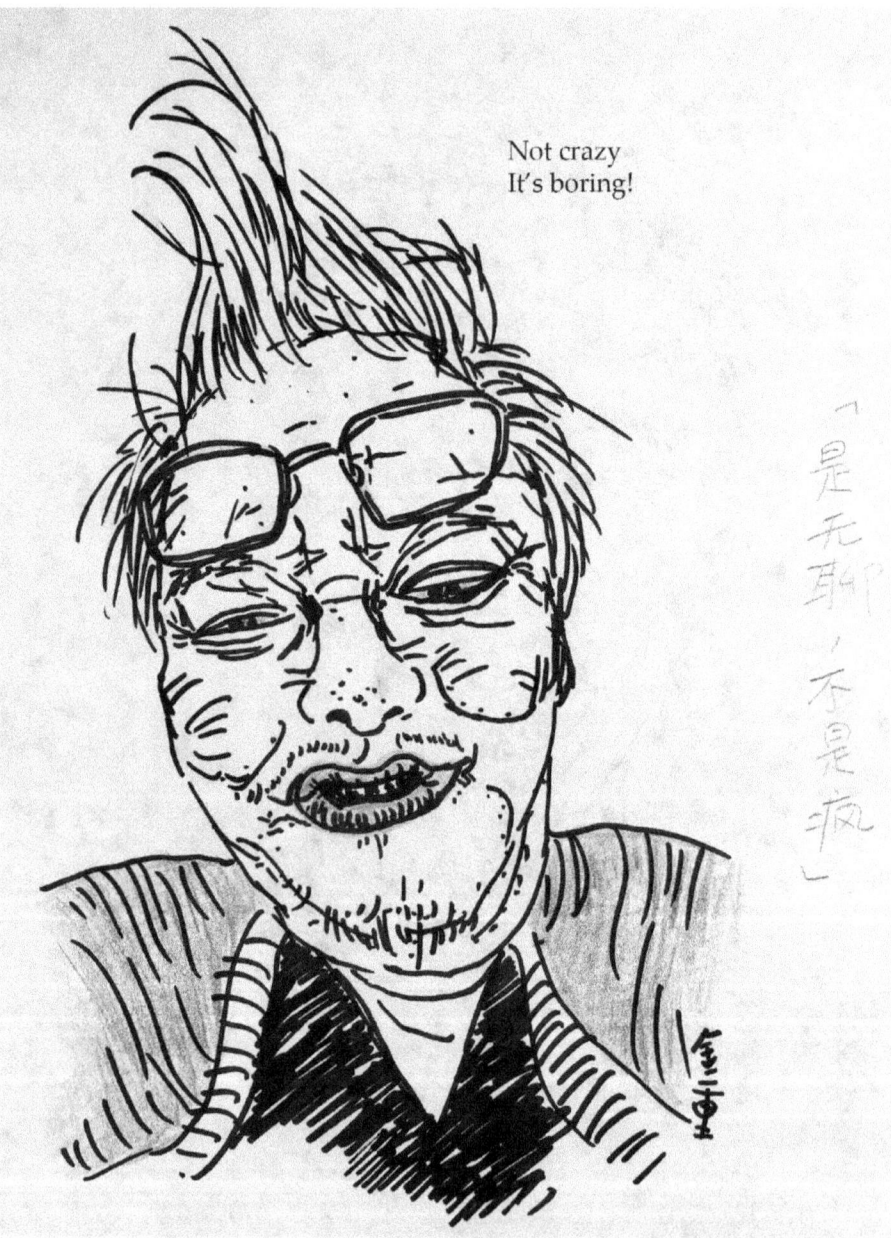

Not crazy
It's boring!

「是无耻，不是疯」

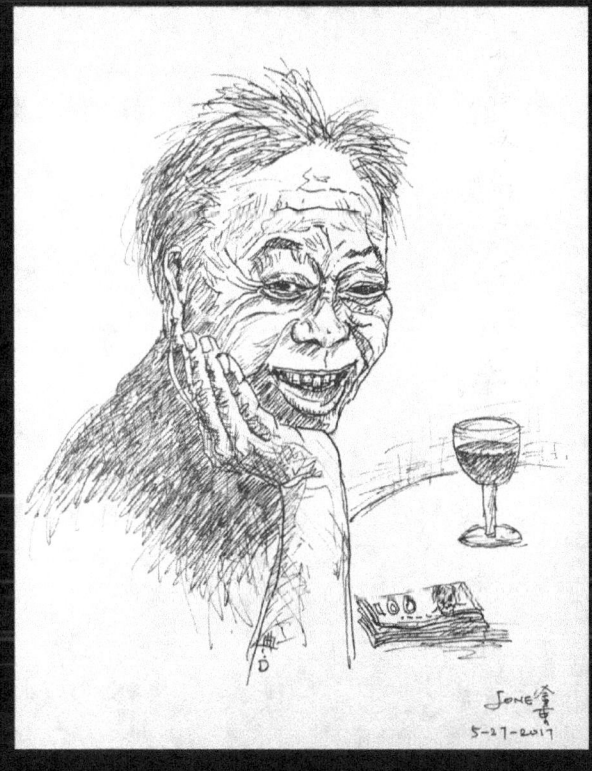

HOPE

I watch TV after dinner
And see many poverty-stricken families
Their kids cannot afford school
I suddenly want to sponsor a child
To go to Hope Elementary
I can do this
If I quit the hookers
For just one time
Each month

Dian Qiu
Translated by Jin Zhong

《希望》典裘

晚上看电视
看到许多穷人家的孩子
没钱上学
我突然也想资助一个孩了
上希望小学
最多是一个月
少嫖一次

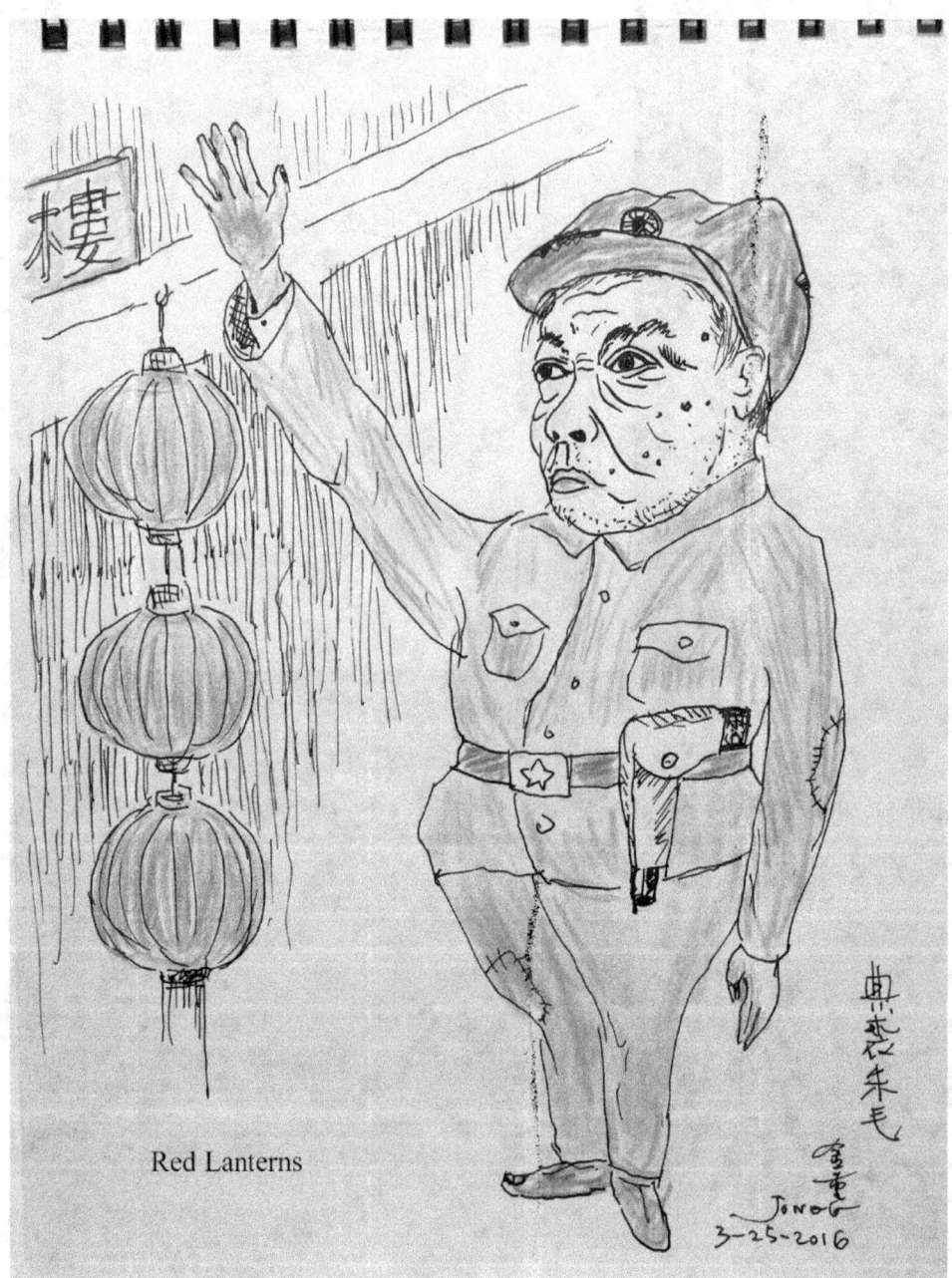

Red Lanterns

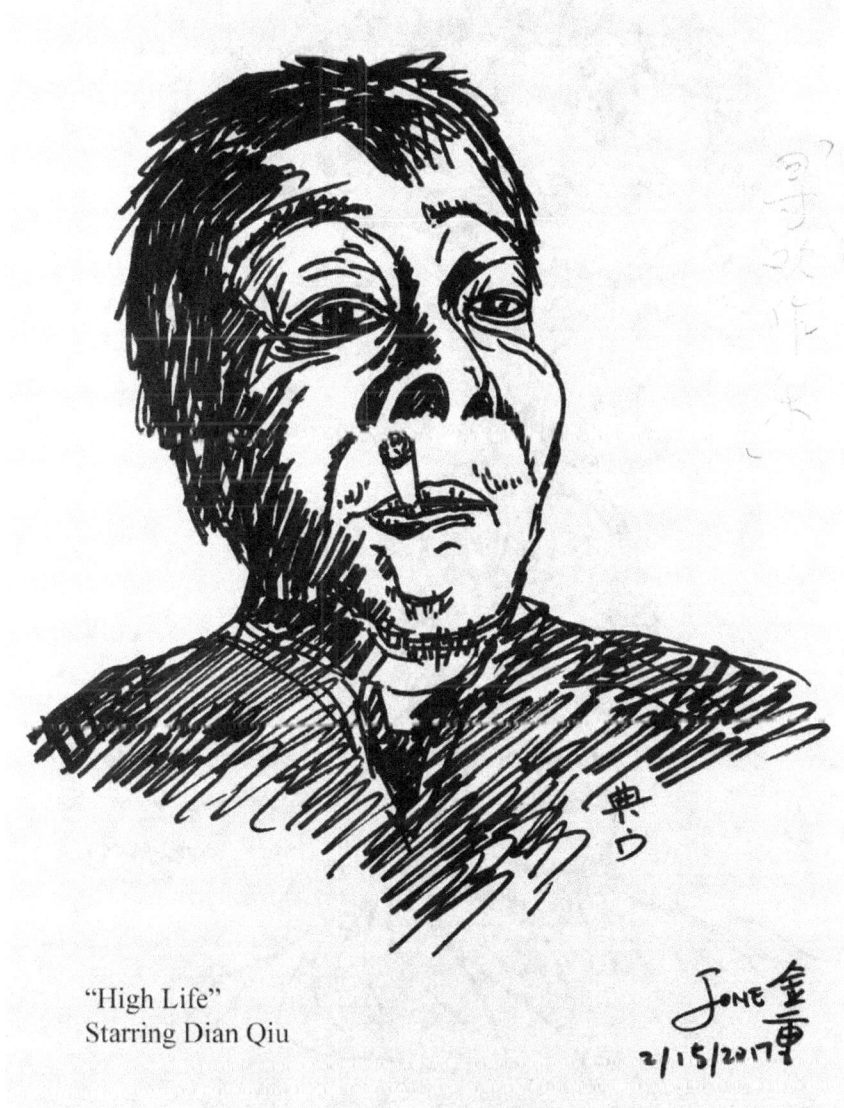

"High Life"
Starring Dian Qiu

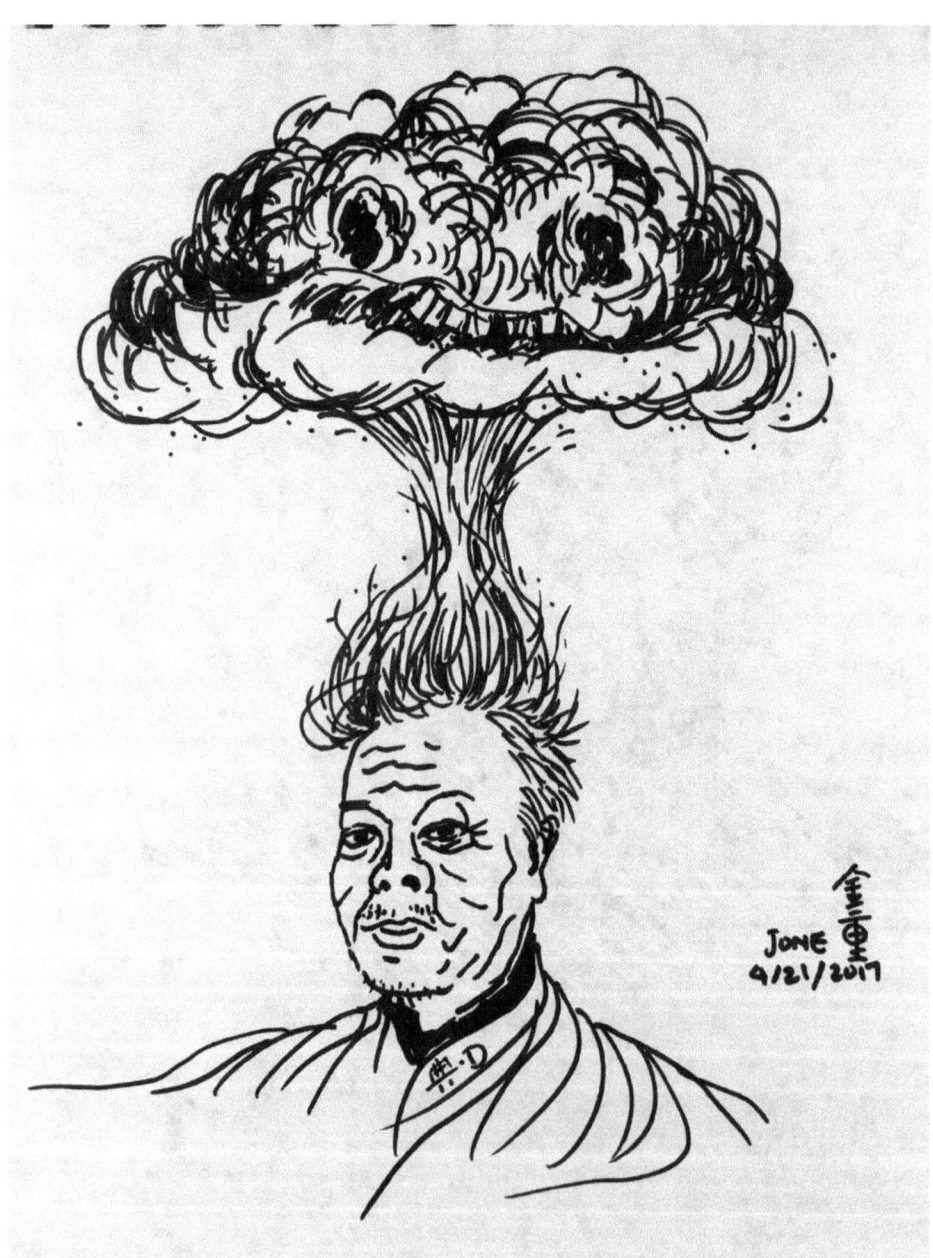

贪官纪念碑　典裘

我在梦中砌了一座贪官纪念碑
与人民英雄纪念碑默默相对
每天都有很多人大骂吐口水扔垃圾
偶尔也有妖艳的女子
悄悄地放上一束玫瑰花

终于有了一座类似雷峰塔的建筑物了
花冈岩真能震住那些丑陋的灵魂吗
这个夏天好象又有什么事件要发生
而真象却要曝光在半个世纪后

夜色中的烈士们
纷纷从浮雕走下去看新的纪念碑
他们向衣冠楚楚的贪官们
敬礼并且叫一声首长好
他们怎能想到这么多首长
会倒在自己人的枪口下
更想不到这是一座贪官纪念碑

烈士们抱着英雄纪念碑痛哭
贪官们趴在权力金钱美女身上痛哭
当一声枪响后，仍然有许多贪官
前赴后继
戴着避孕套
深入祖国的体内

从故宫飞出了一群乌鸦
惊醒了我的梦
不知道在以后的梦里
我是拆除这座纪念碑
还是用贪官的骨头砌一座长城

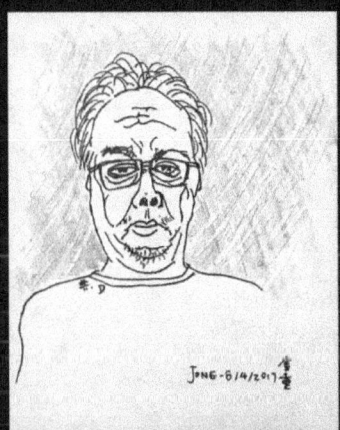

Dian Qiu,
pen name of
Shen Shaoqiu
born in 1959

policer officer
leader of trash poetry
movie star

MONUMENT TO THE CORRUPT OFFICIALS

MONUMENT TO THE CORRUPT OFFICIALS

In my dream I build a monument to the corrupt officials
It quietly watches the Monument to the People's Heroes
Across the square
Everyday people will curse, spit, throw trash to it
Some sexy lady will sneak in
She will lay a bouquet of roses

Now at last we have something like the Leifeng Pagoda
Can granite overwhelm those ugly souls?
Is something evil about to happen again when summer is here?
But the world wouldn't learn it half a century from now

At nightfall the dead soldiers jump down from the relief
They stand in line to watch the new monument
They salute to the pretentious corrupt officials
They shout "hi, Commander" that echoes in the square
But they don't know these officials
Are executed by their own comrades
They don't know
This monument is a monument of shame

The dead soldiers cry loud
Their arms against the Monument to the People's Heroes
The corrupt officials cry loud over power, money, and their mistresses
When the gun is fired, more corrupt officials will come to fill the space
They put on condoms, thrust into the body of their motherland

A flock of crows fly out from the Palace Museum
It wakes me up
I don't know what I should do when I go back into this dream:
Do I abolish this monument
Or collect enough bones from the corrupt officials
To build another Great Wall?

Dian Qiu
Translated by Jin Zhong

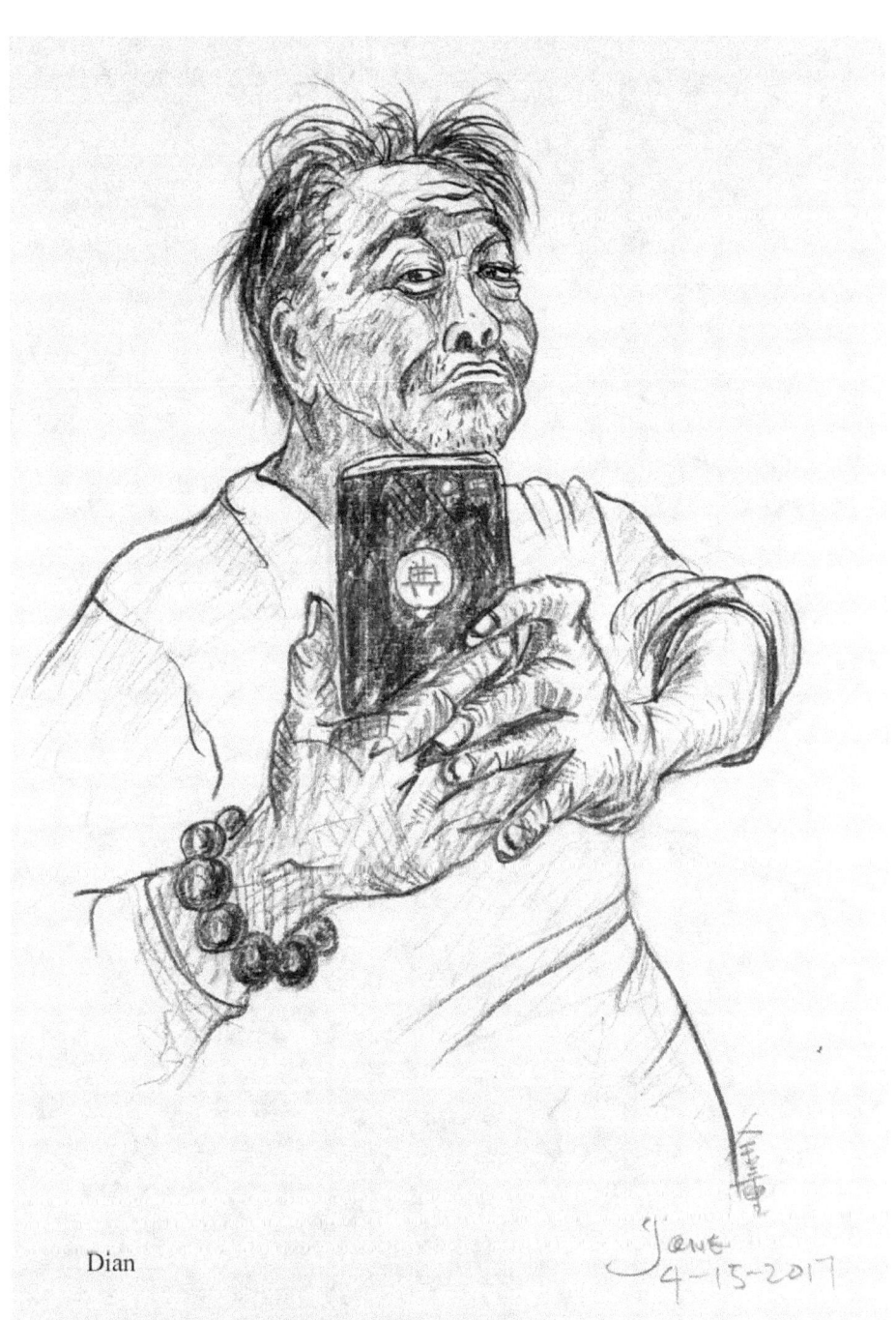

Dian

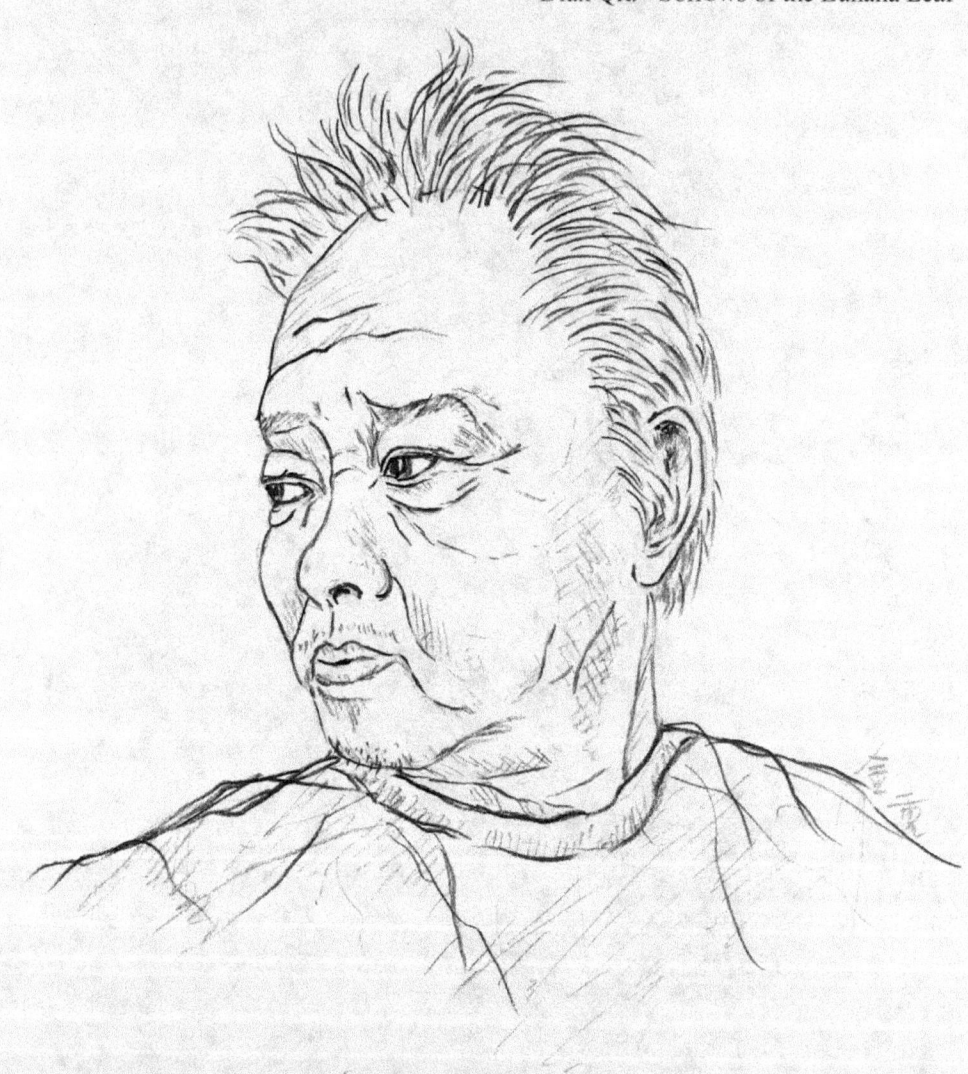

奥震－芭蕉的忧伤

Jone G. San Diego
7-30-2016

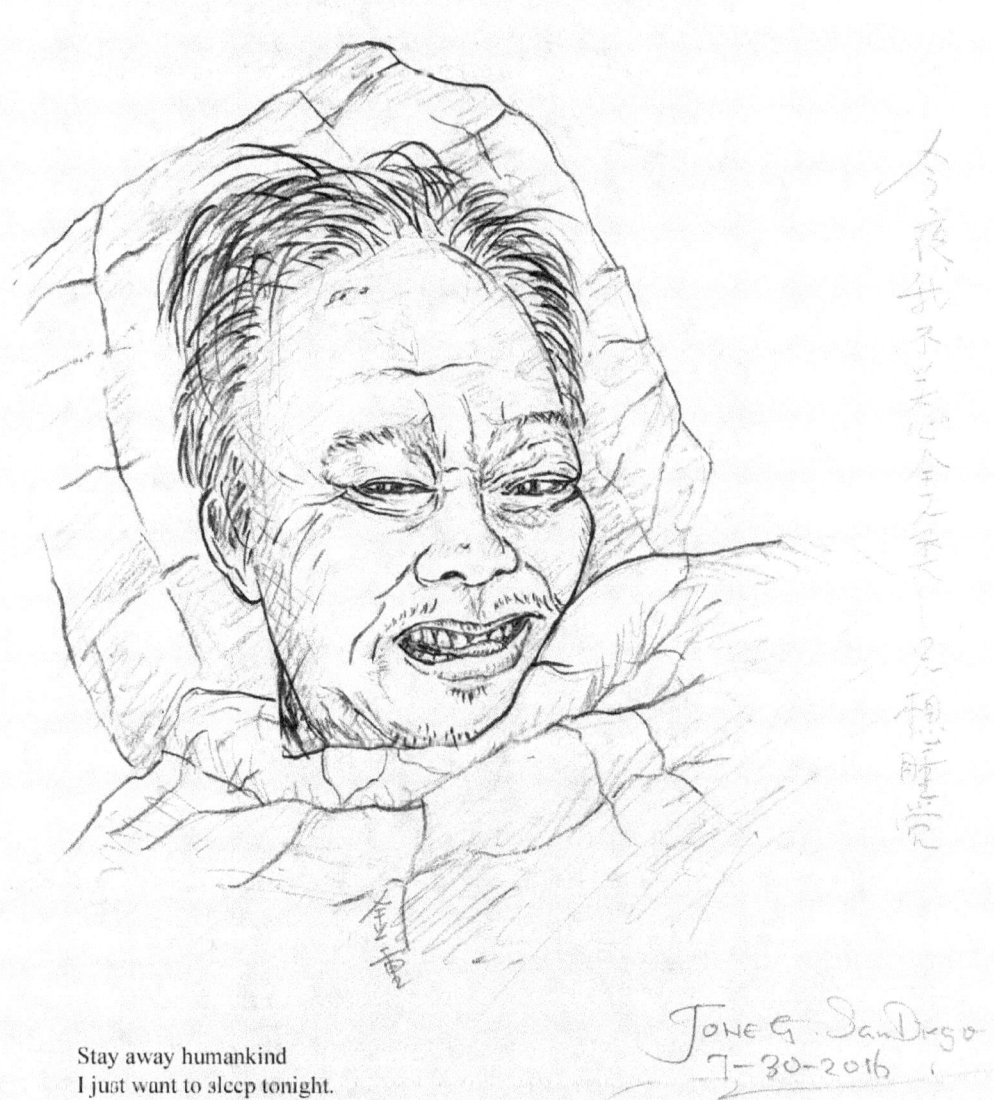

今夜だけは誰からも邪魔されずに眠りたい

Stay away humankind
I just want to sleep tonight.

Jone G. SanDiego
7-30-2016

The horozon
It can block the rise of the sun
It can block the fall of the moon
It can never block the tide of love
　--Dian Qiu

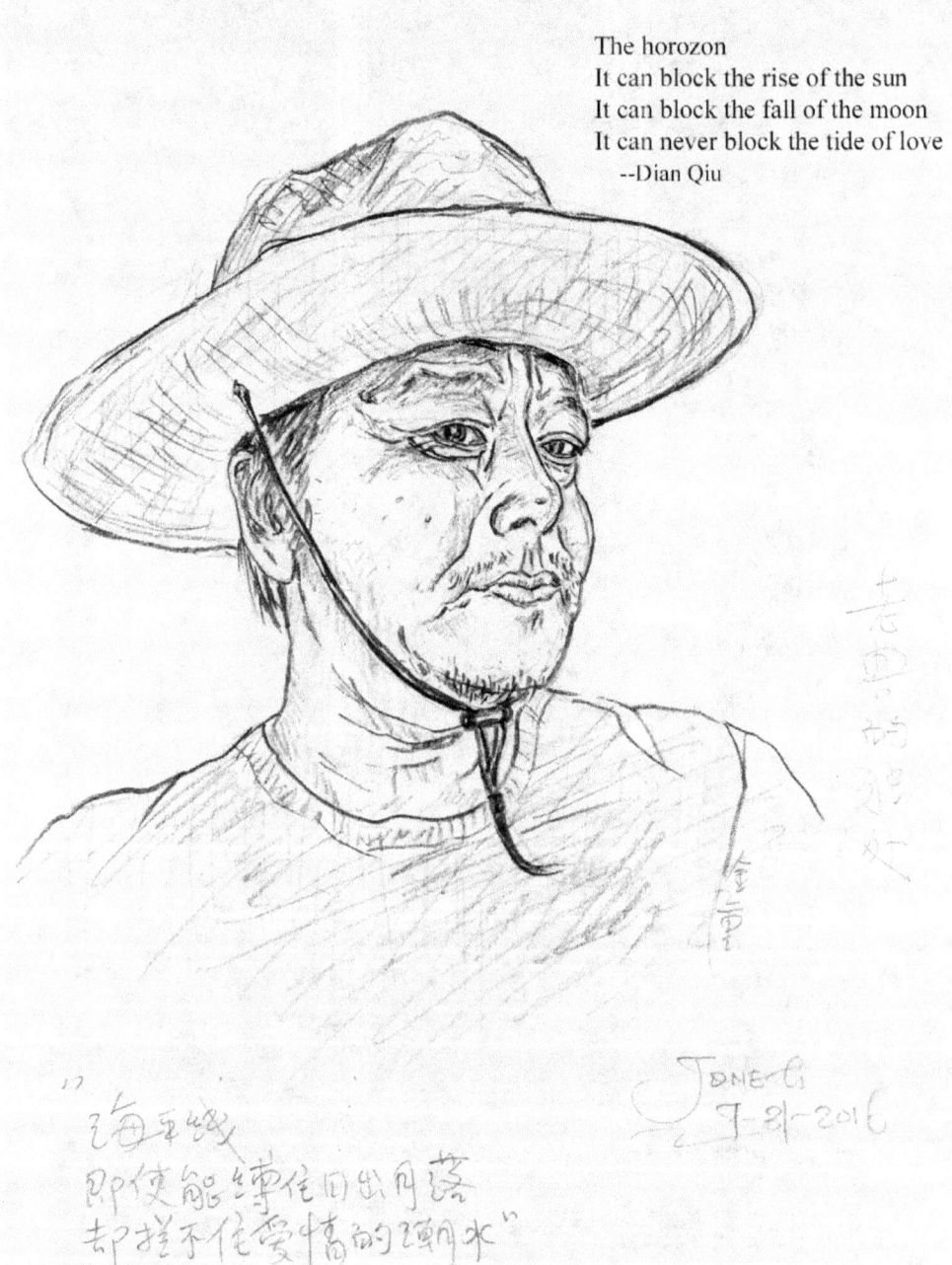

"海平线
即使能够佳日出月落
却挡不住爱情的潮水"

JONE·G
丁酉-2016

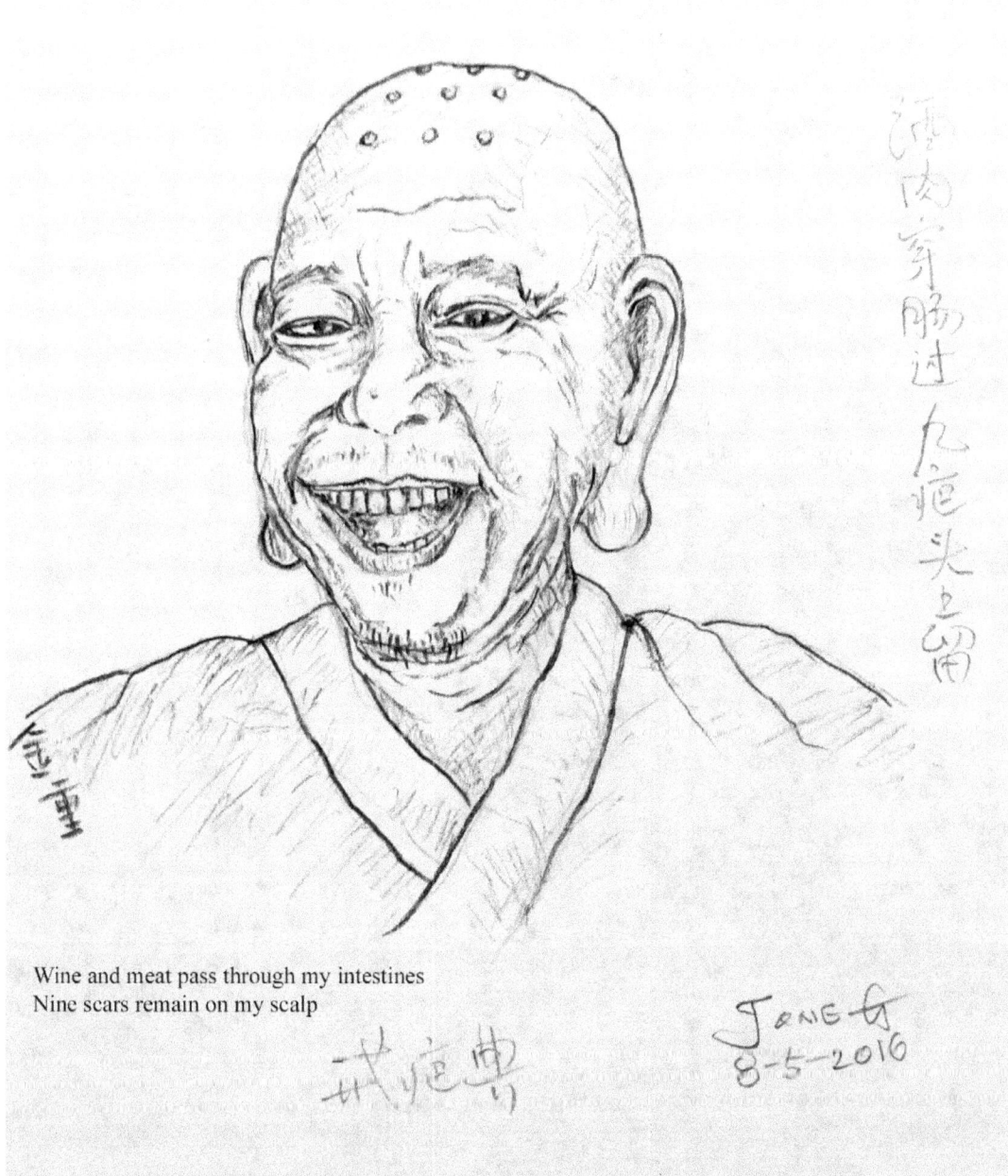

酒肉穿肠过 九疤头上留

Wine and meat pass through my intestines
Nine scars remain on my scalp

戒疤曹

JONE G
8-5-2016

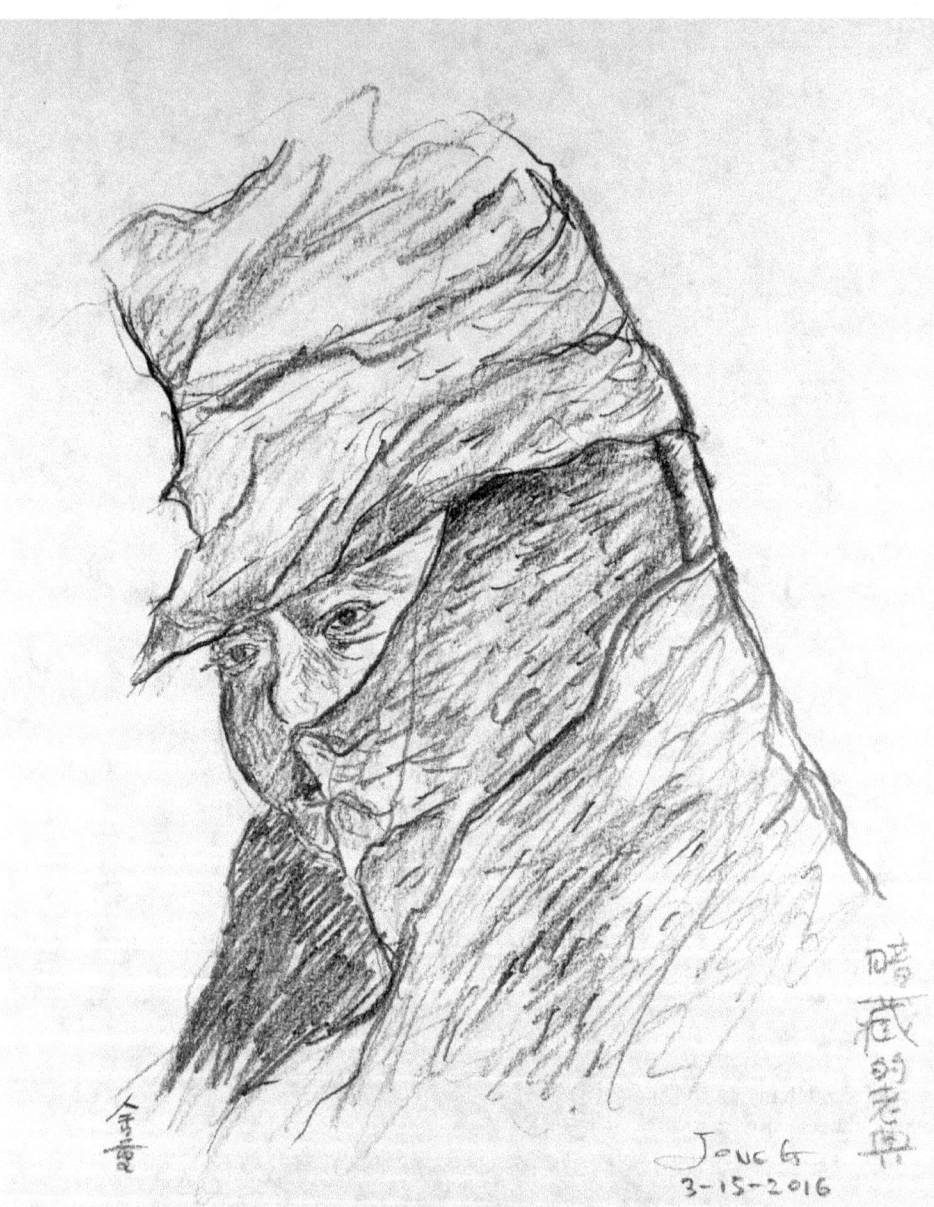

Hidden Old Dian

寻找

十九万八千九百六十四只白鸽
从广场起飞
就有一百万枪口对着天空

我们不是在黑暗中寻找光明
我们是在光明中寻找自由

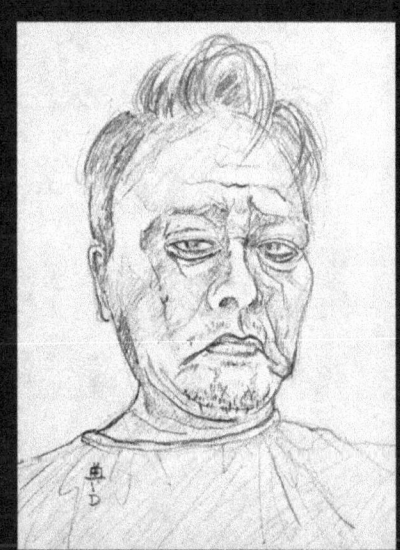

典裘沽酒 2017.7.14.

SEEKING

198,964 white doves
Take off from the square
1,000,000 guns aiming at the sky

We are not seeking the light in darkness
We are seeking freedom in the light

July 14, 2017

Dian Qiu
Translated by Jin Zhong

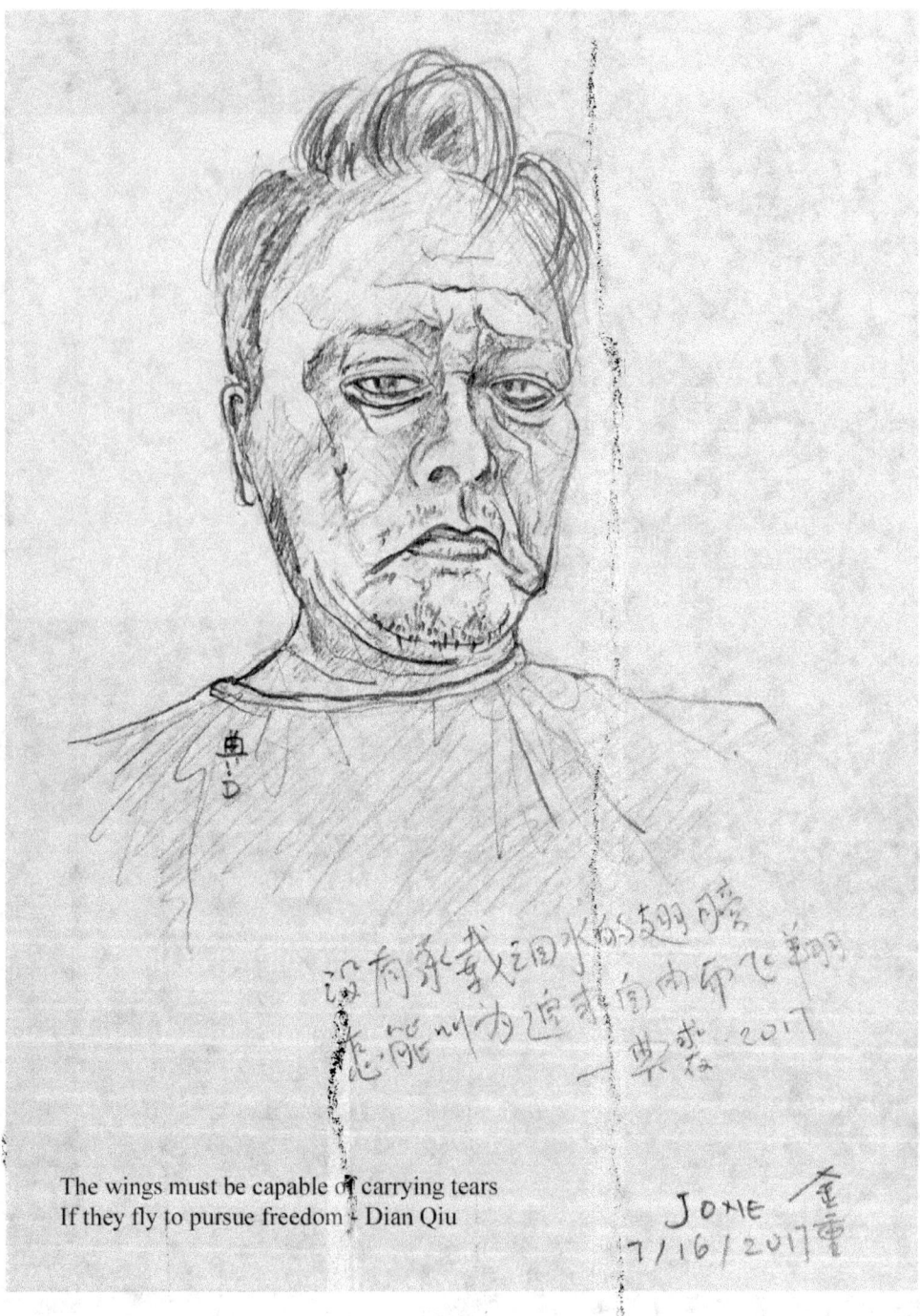

没有泪水我回水
忘

The wings must be capable of carrying tears
If they fly to pursue freedom - Dian Qiu

JONE 金
7/16/2017

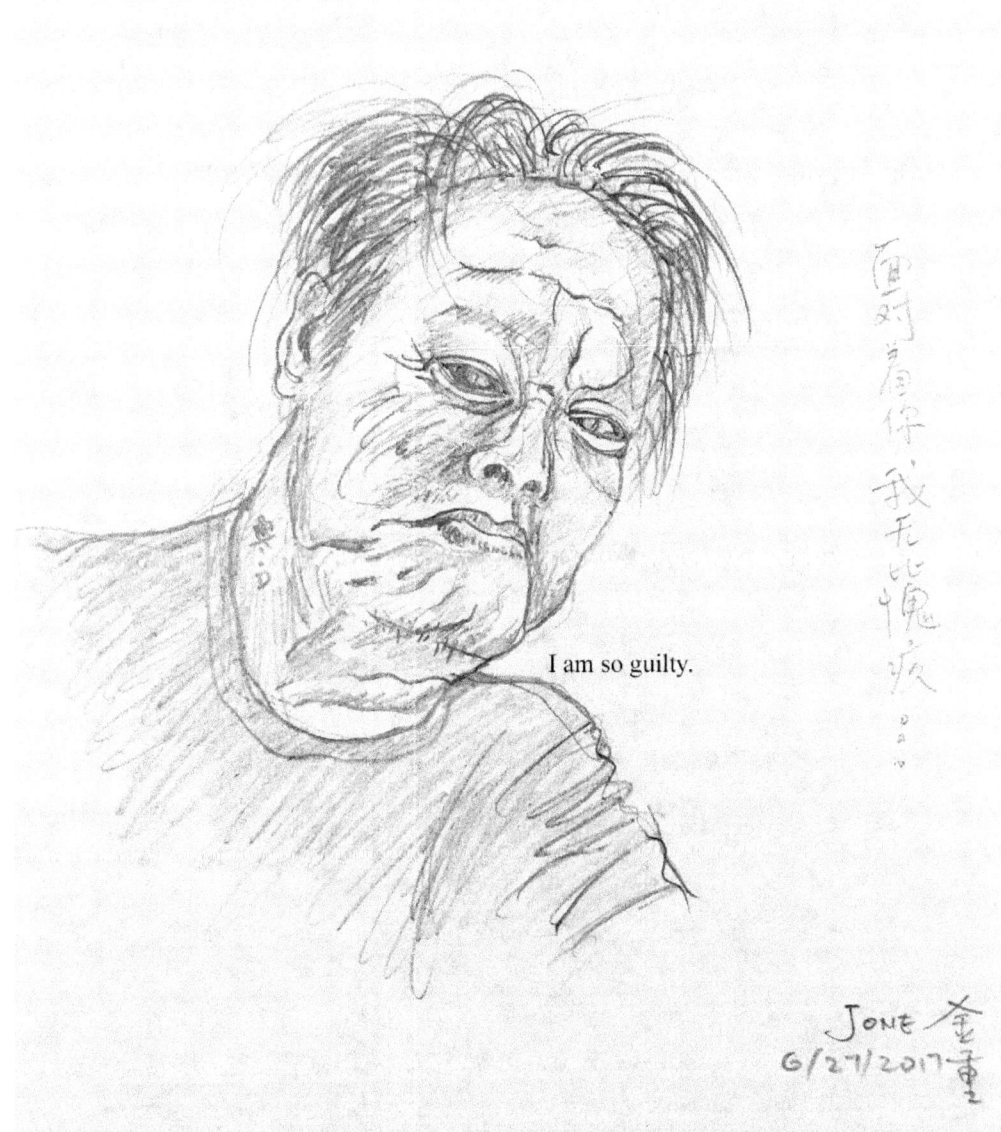

I am so guilty.

面对着你 我无愧疚。。

JONE 金重
6/27/2017

La grande tristesse du poète

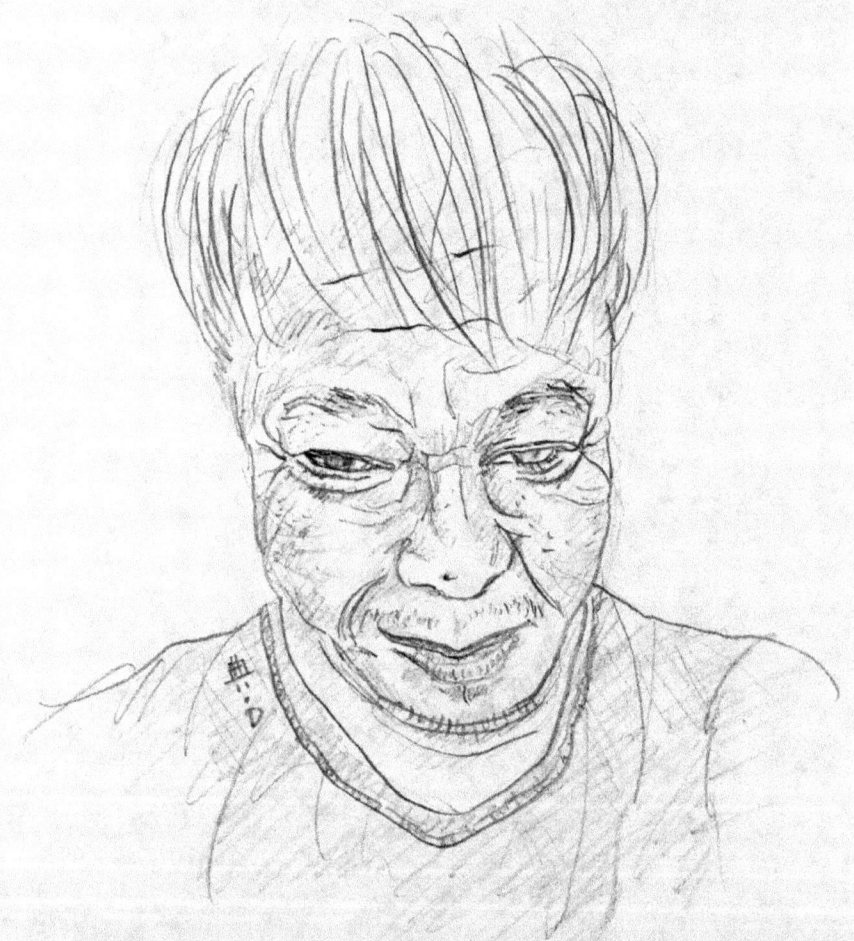

The great sadness of the poet

Jane 7/10/2017

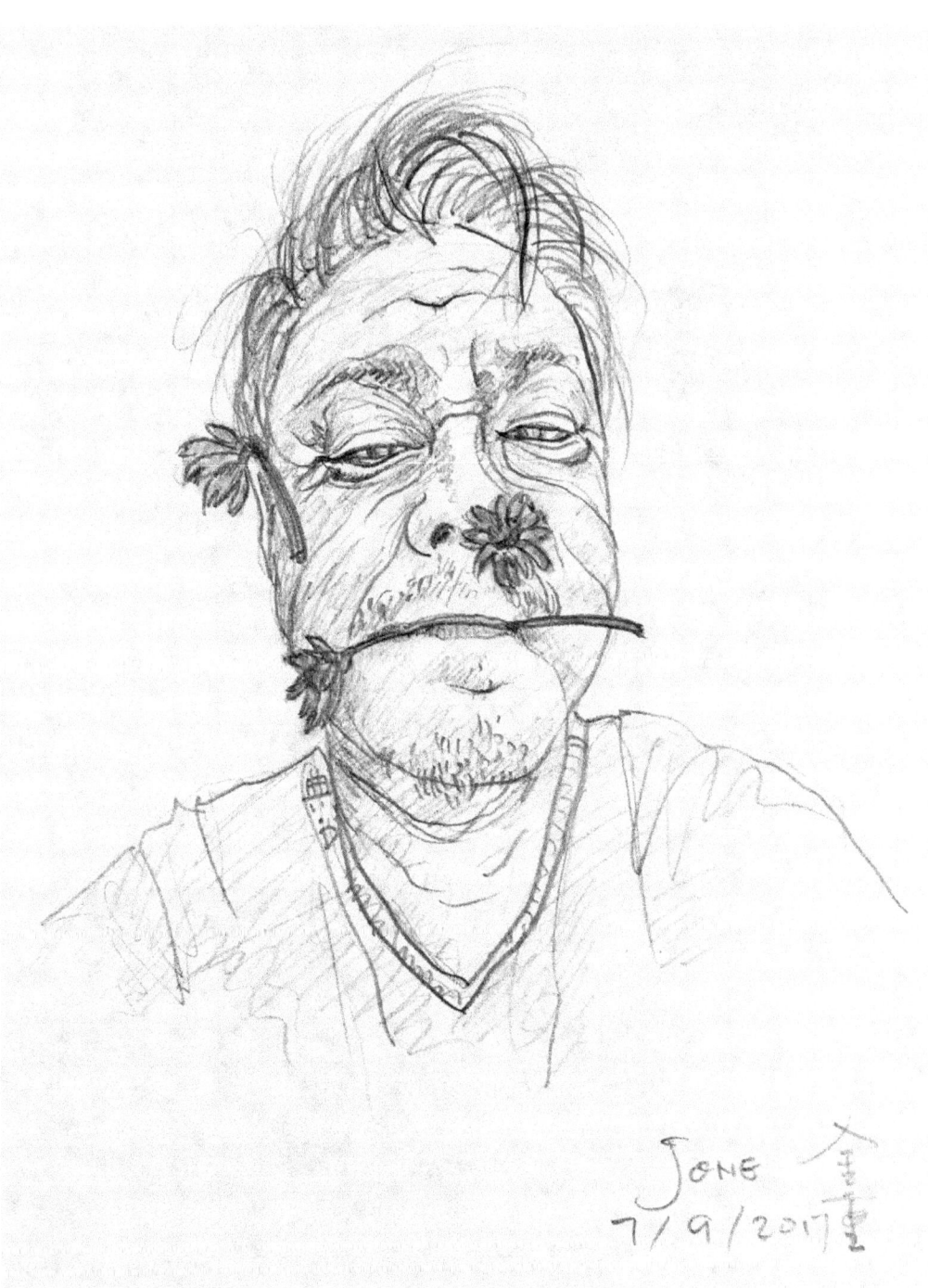

JONE 金
7/9/2017畫

Dian Qiu the Rightist

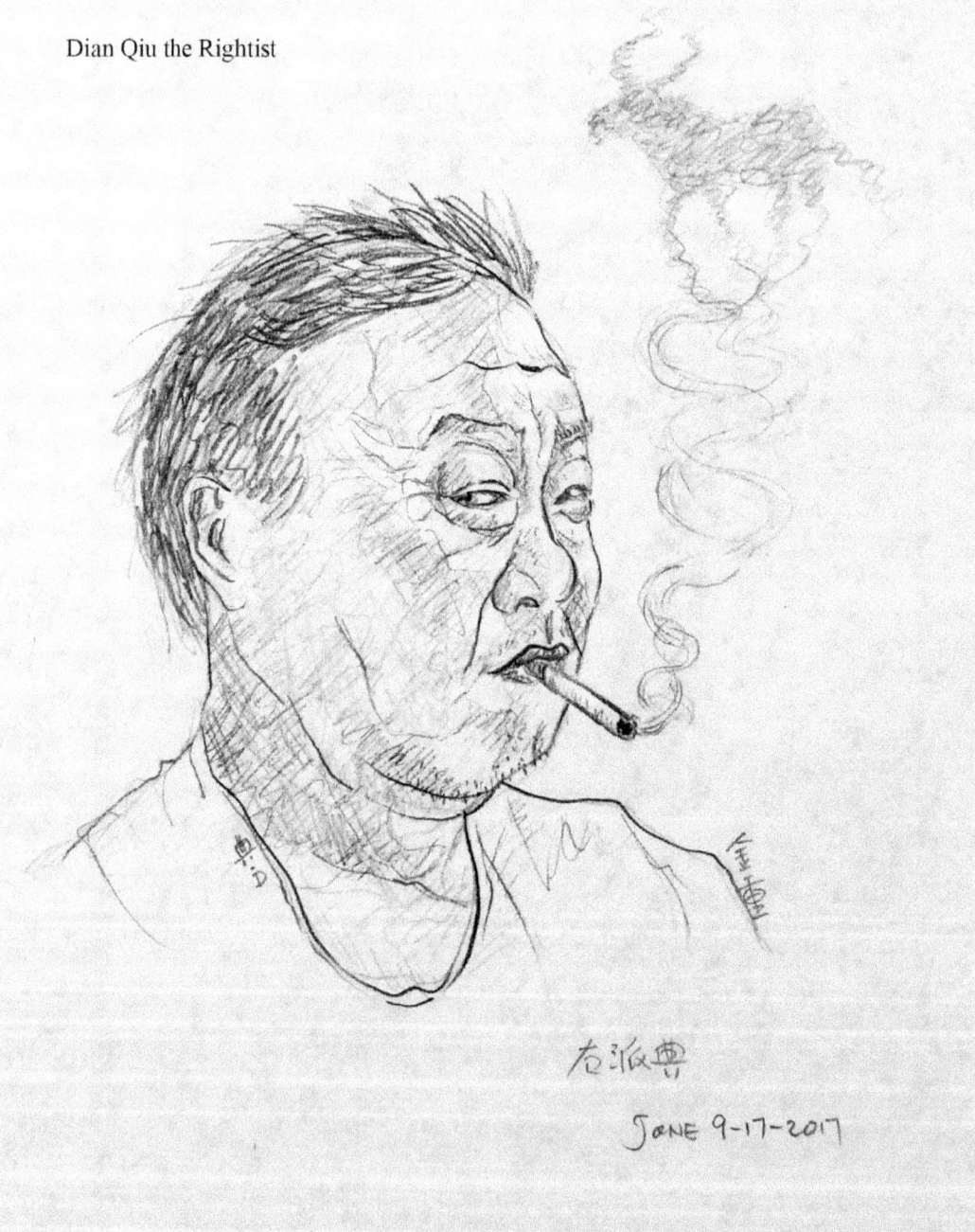

右派曹

JUNE 9-17-2017

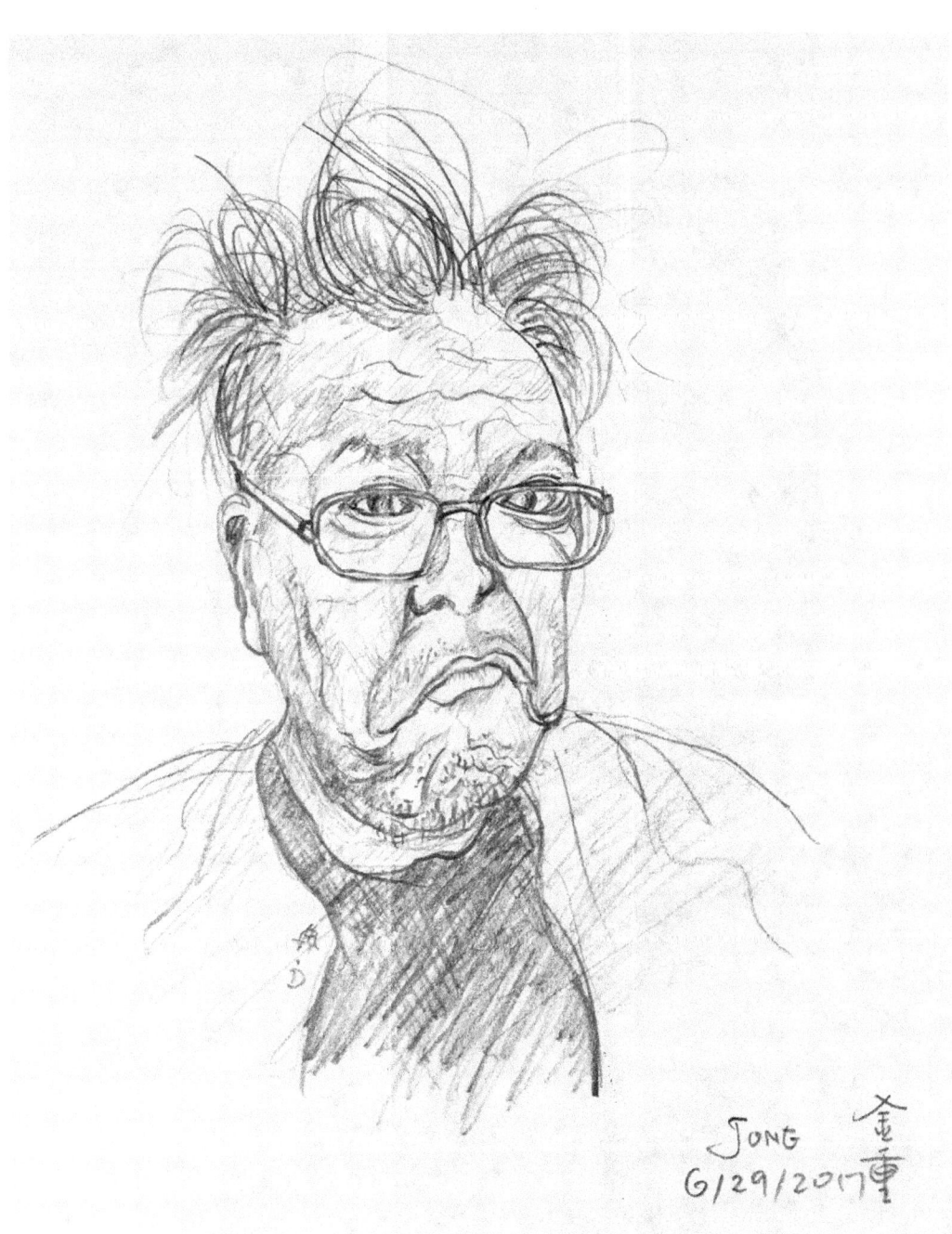

JONG
6/29/2017 金重

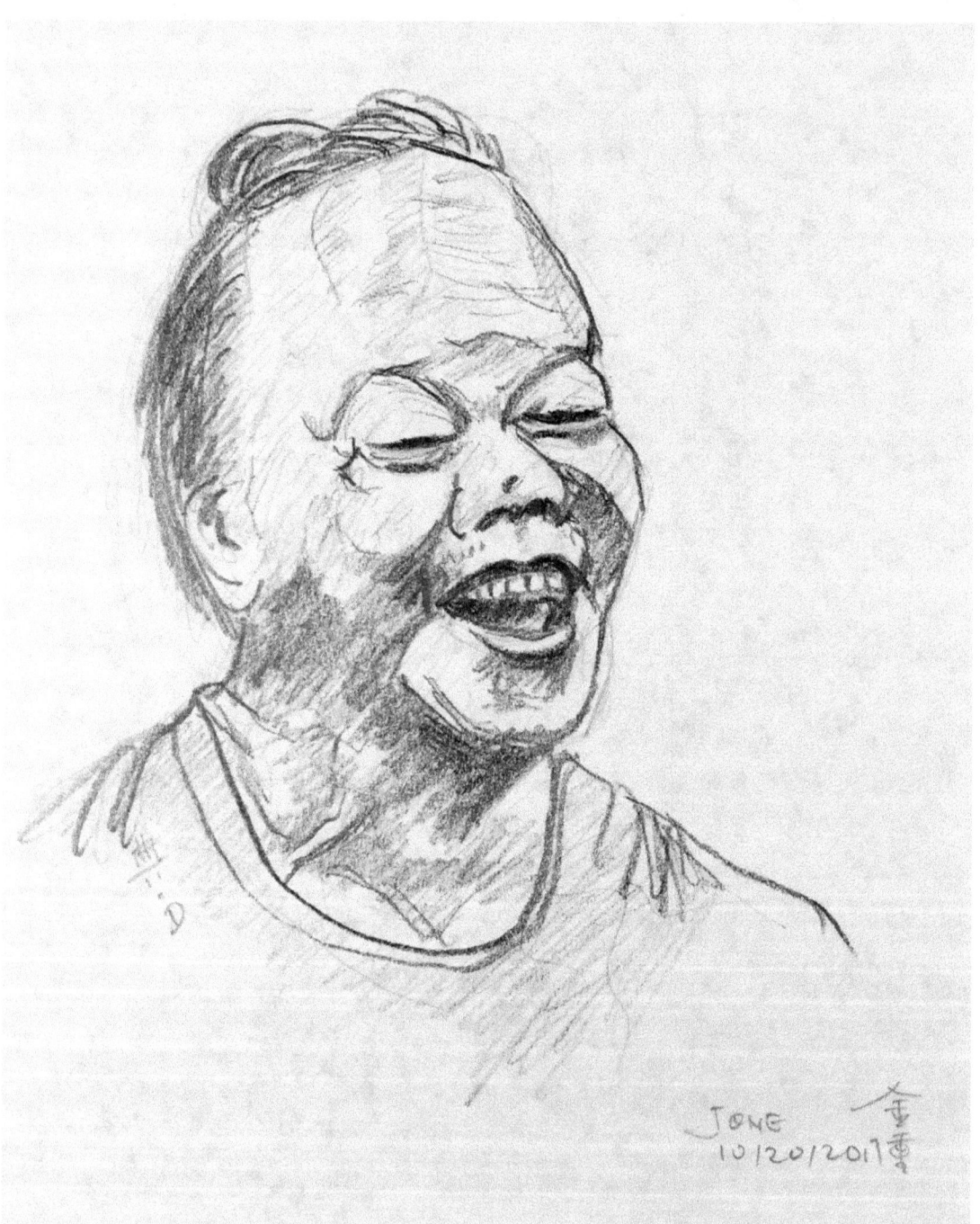

JONE
10/20/2011

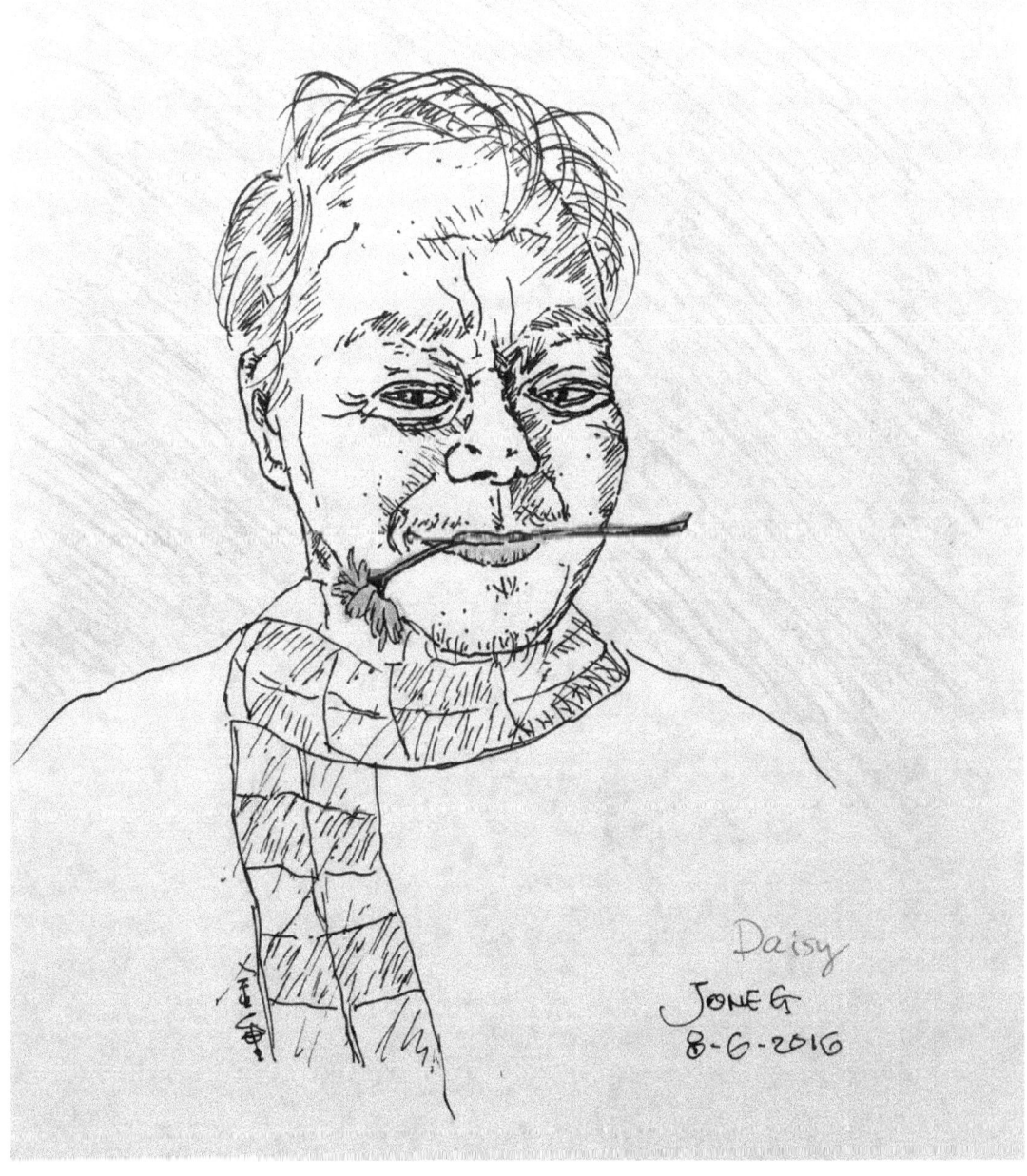

Daisy
JONE G
8-6-2016

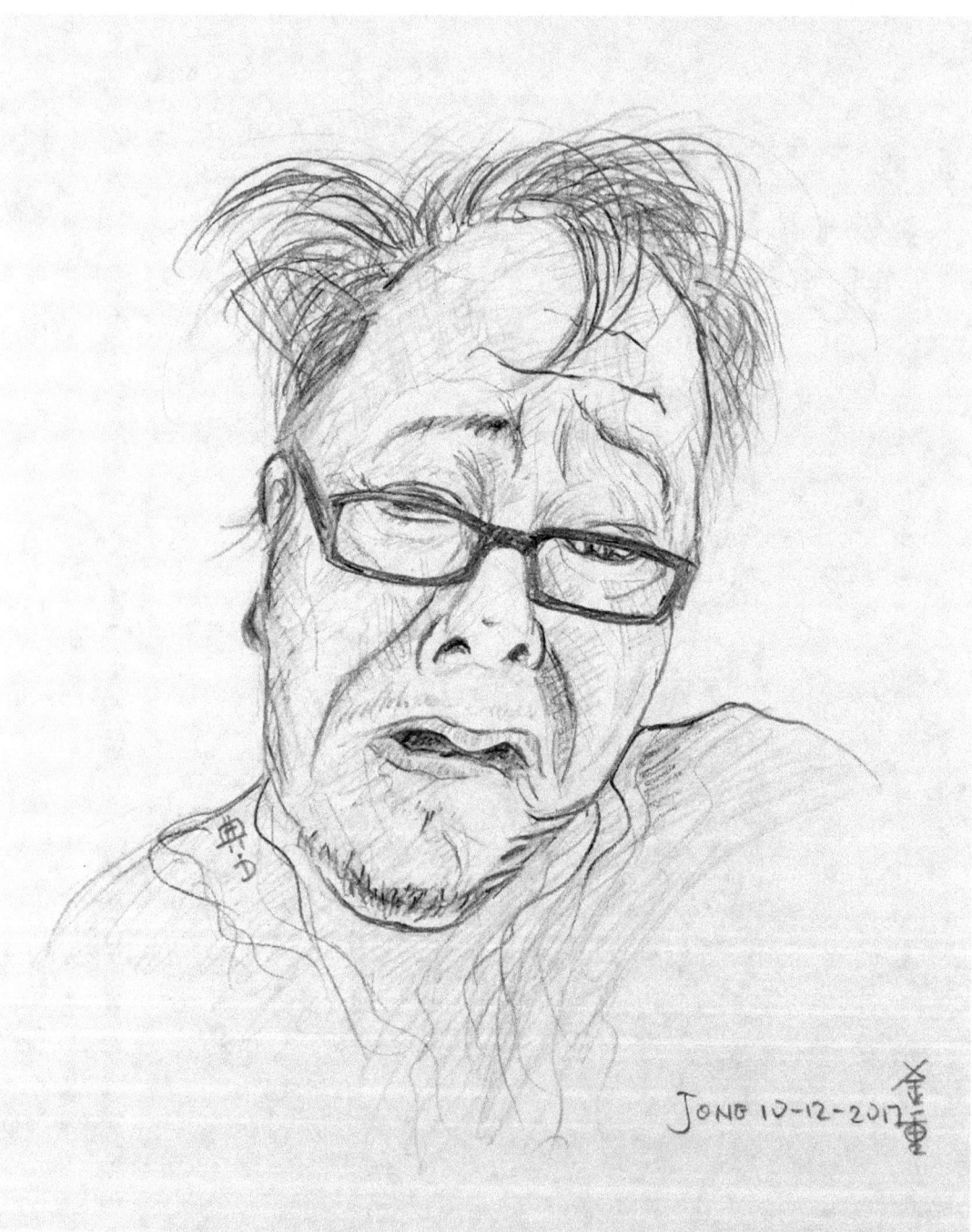

JONG 10-12-2017

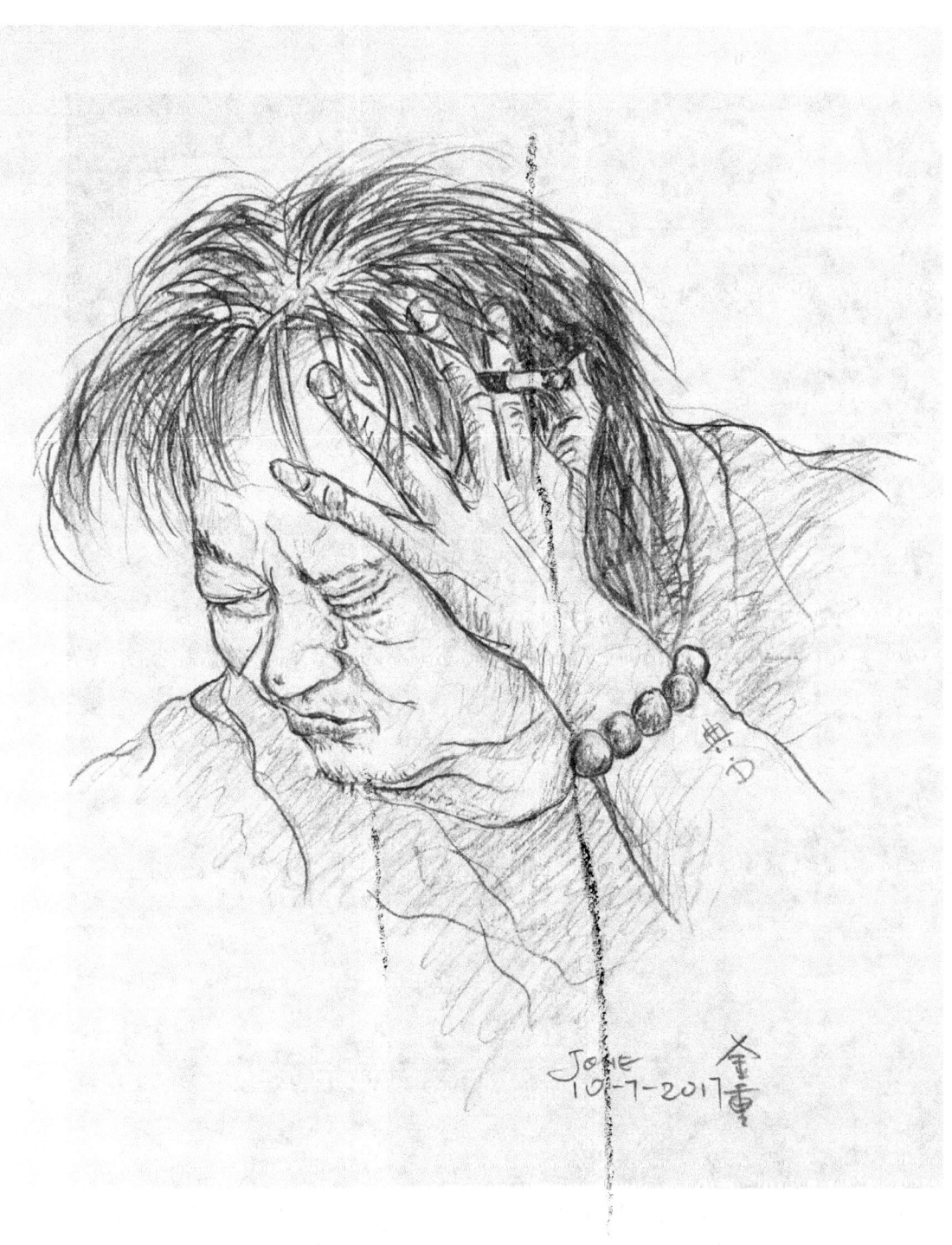

Jone
10-7-2011

猫　典裘

一列火车开过
一只猫蹲在高墙上
黄昏将尽的天空
两只眼睛
格外的蓝

猫的眼里
排列着许多铁栏杆
许多人在动
它不懂
它是在铁栏杆里面
还是栏杆外面

又一列火车开过
猫不见了

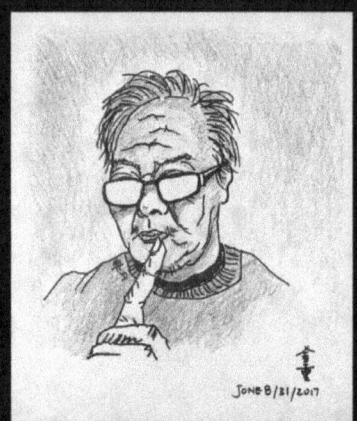

CAT

A train hurls past
A cat crouches
On the high wall
In the darkening dusk
His two eyes glow
With bewildering blue

In the cat's eyes
Iron bars form a long fence
People shift
Many people
Cat cannot tell
If he is behind those bars
Or just in front of them

Another train hurls past
The cat vanishes

Dian Qiu
Translated by Jin Zhong

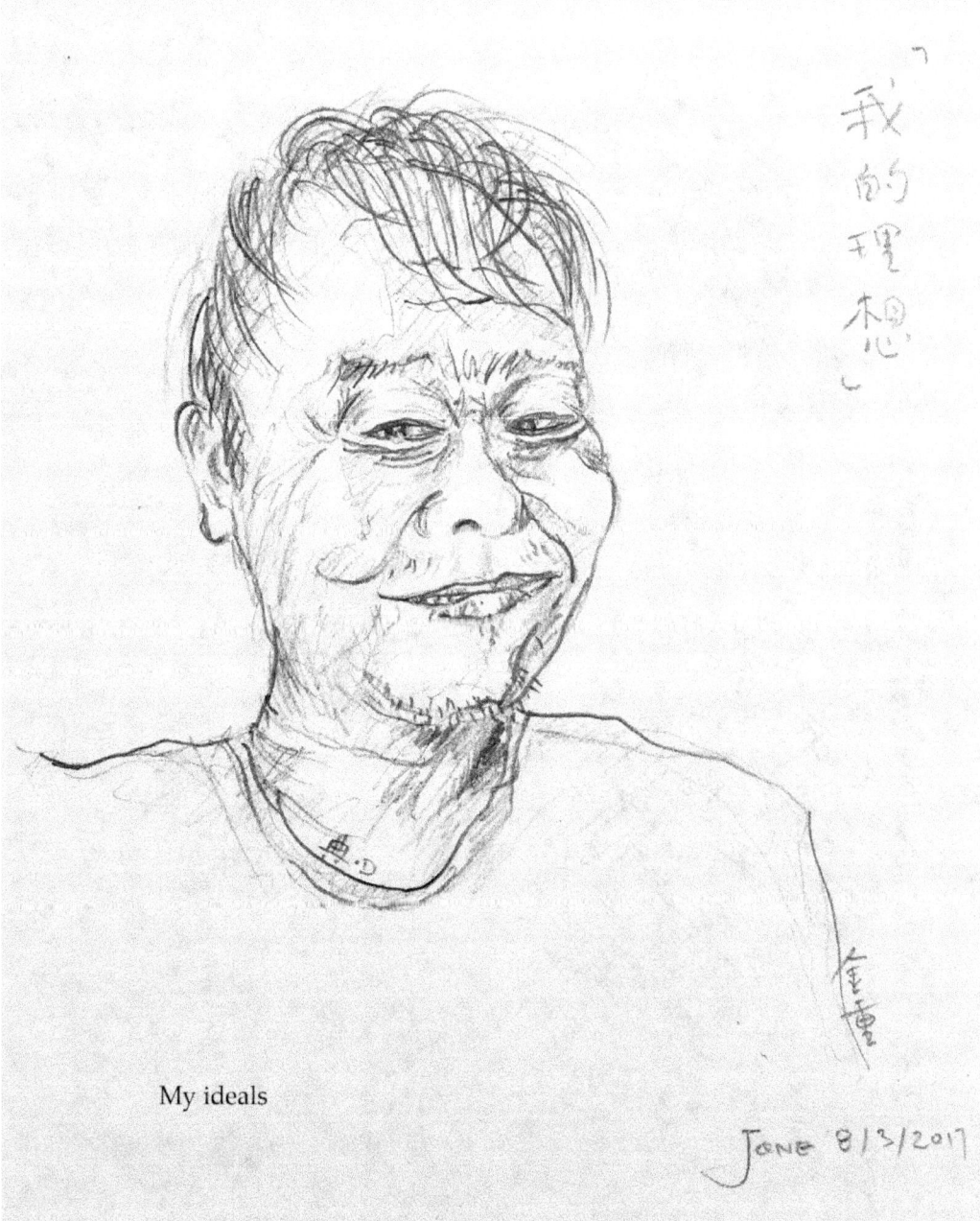

「我的理想」

My ideals

金重

Jane 8/3/2017

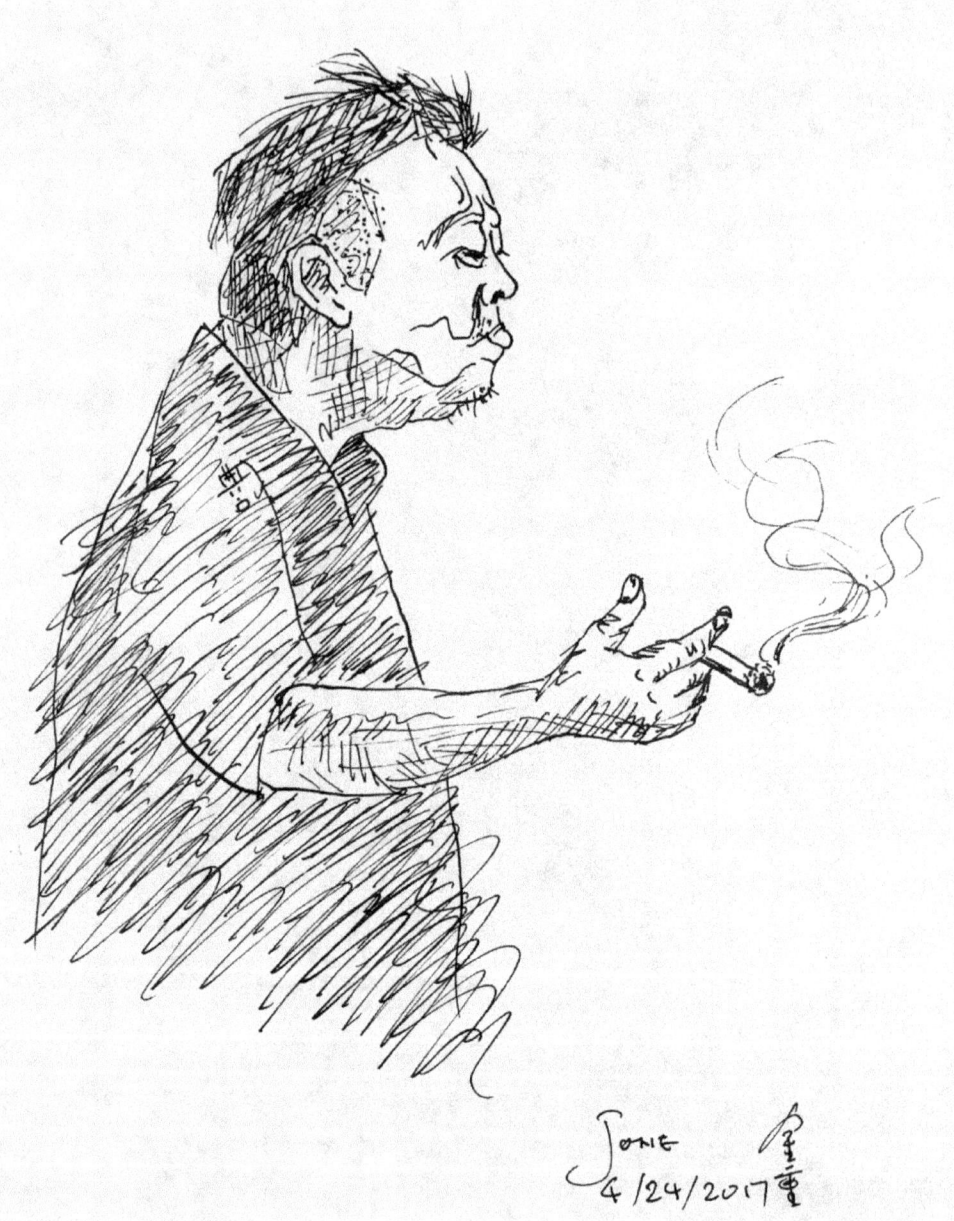

Jone
4/24/2017

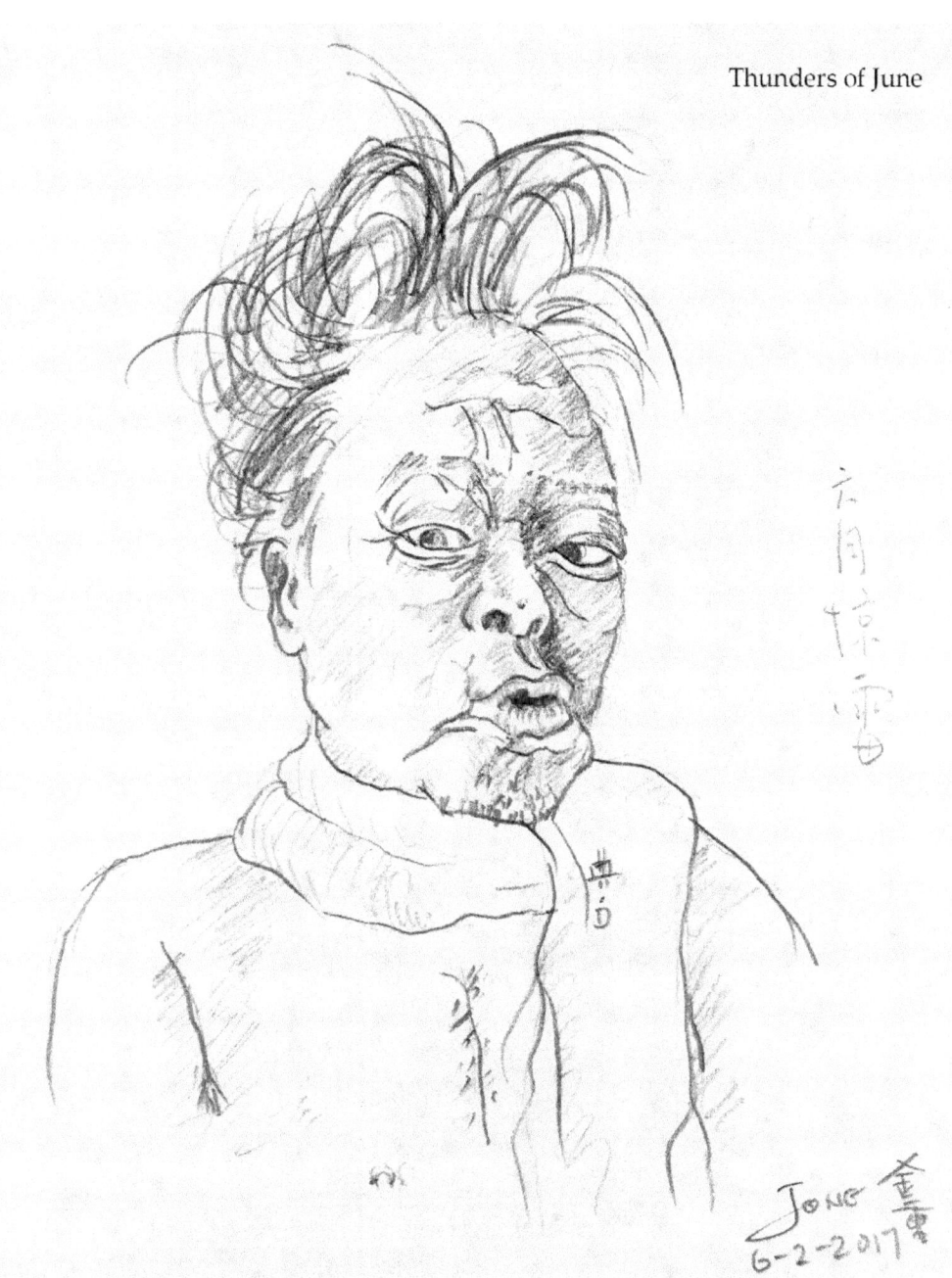

六月驚雷

Jong 金書
6-2-2017

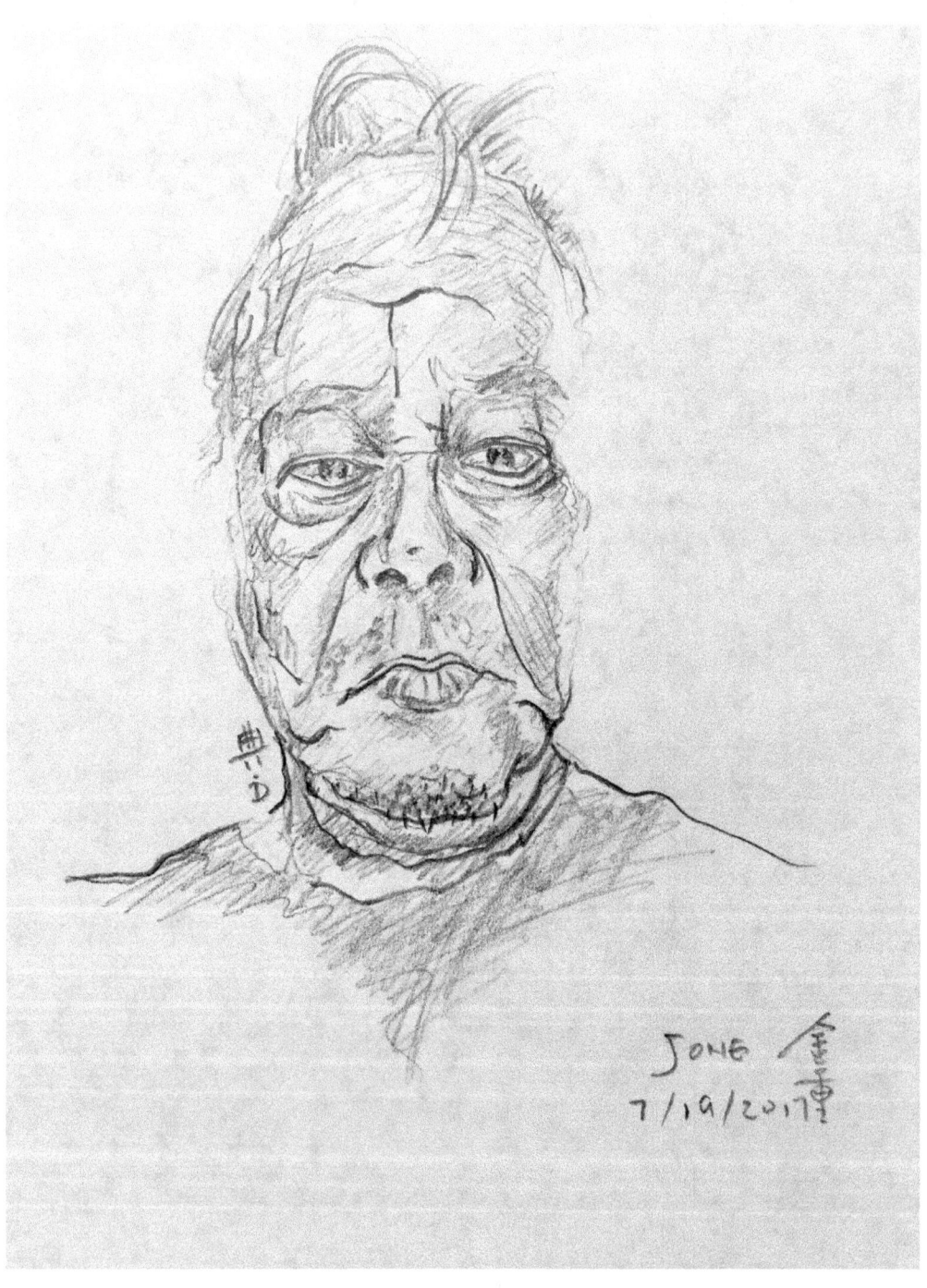

JONG 金重
7/19/2017

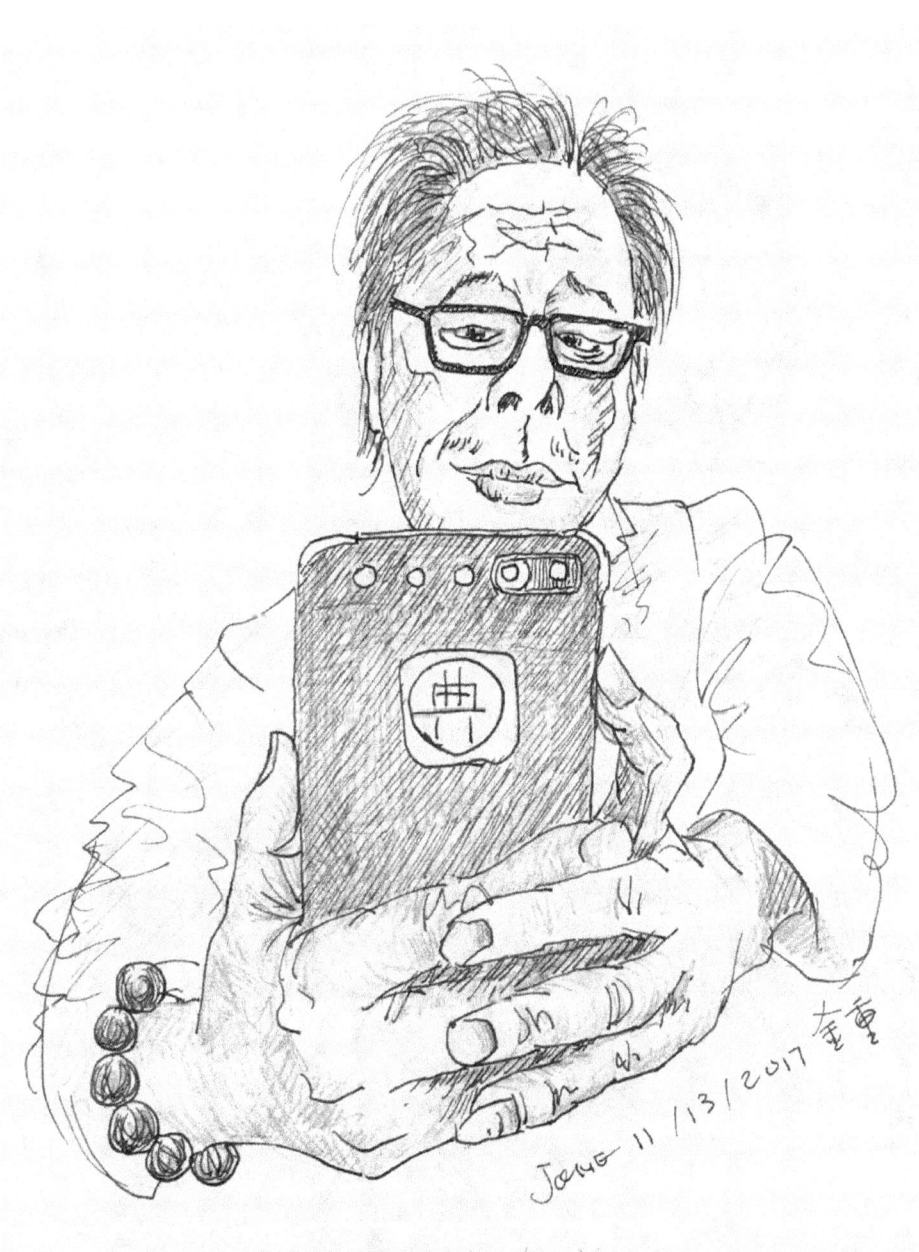

June 11/13/2017 奎重

典裁红引！

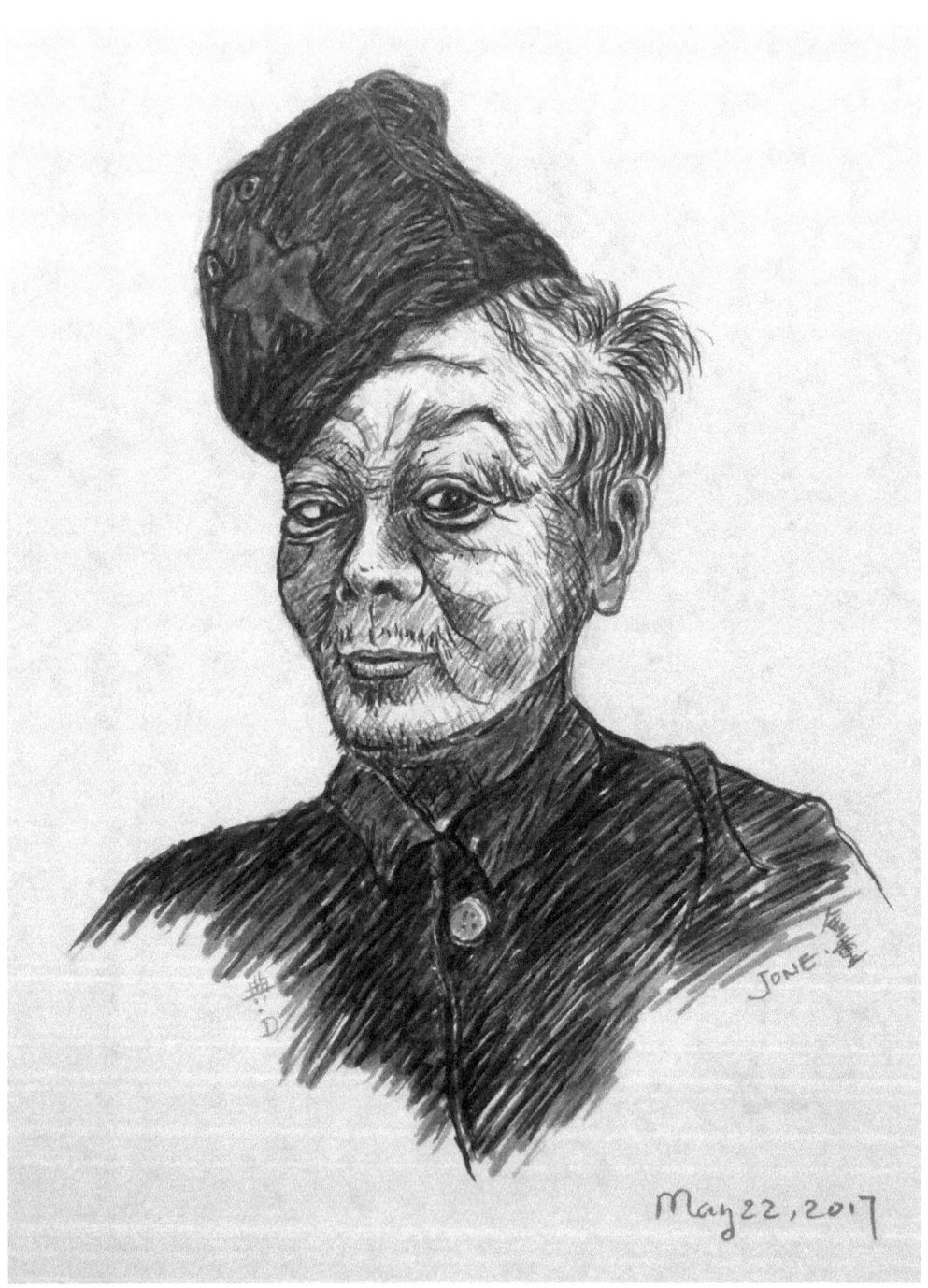

JONE·金童

May 22, 2017

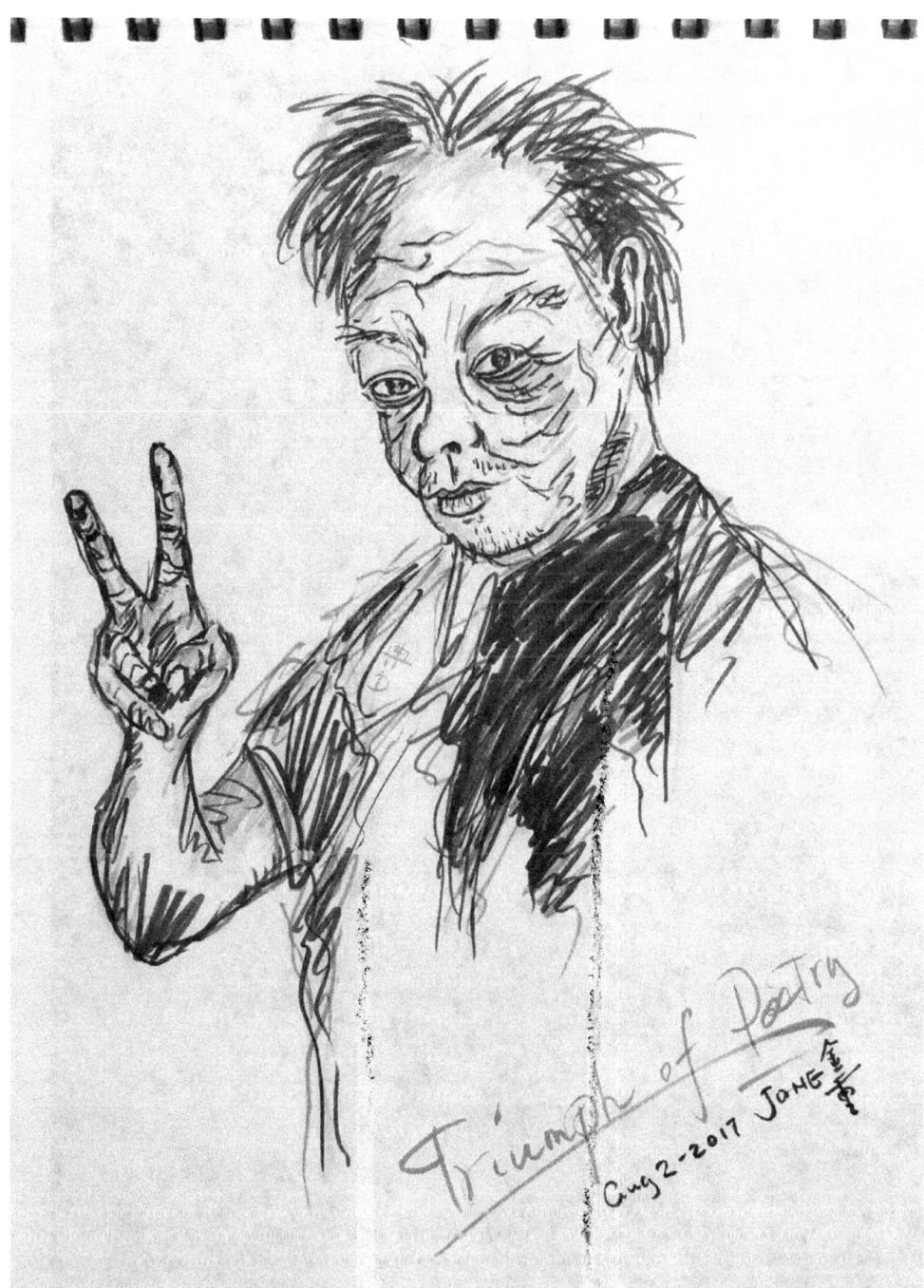

Triumph of Poetry

Aug 2-2017 JONG 金書

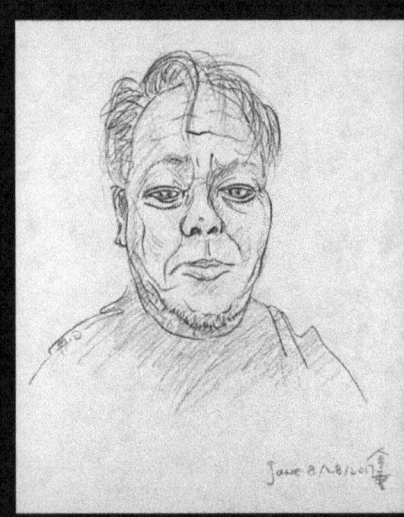

年轮　　典裘

蚊香
一生的激情
一夜就燃尽
回忆
却是灰的年轮

涟漪
一小石子
鱼虾戏水
就能泛起
只是一瞬间
倒影
也变形

树
一圈一圈
拥抱岁月
直到被锯断
才能看到
年轮
雕刻在骨头里

Growth Rings

Mosquito coils
Passion of a life
Burn away in one night
Memory
Is but some ashes of growth rings

Ripples
Can be created by a tiny stone
Or a jumping fish
In one instant
Reflections
Are disturbed

The tree
Ring after ring
Embraces the years
Until it is sawed in half
Growth rings are revealed
Growth rings are carved
In your bones

Dian Qiu
Trans. by Jin Zhong

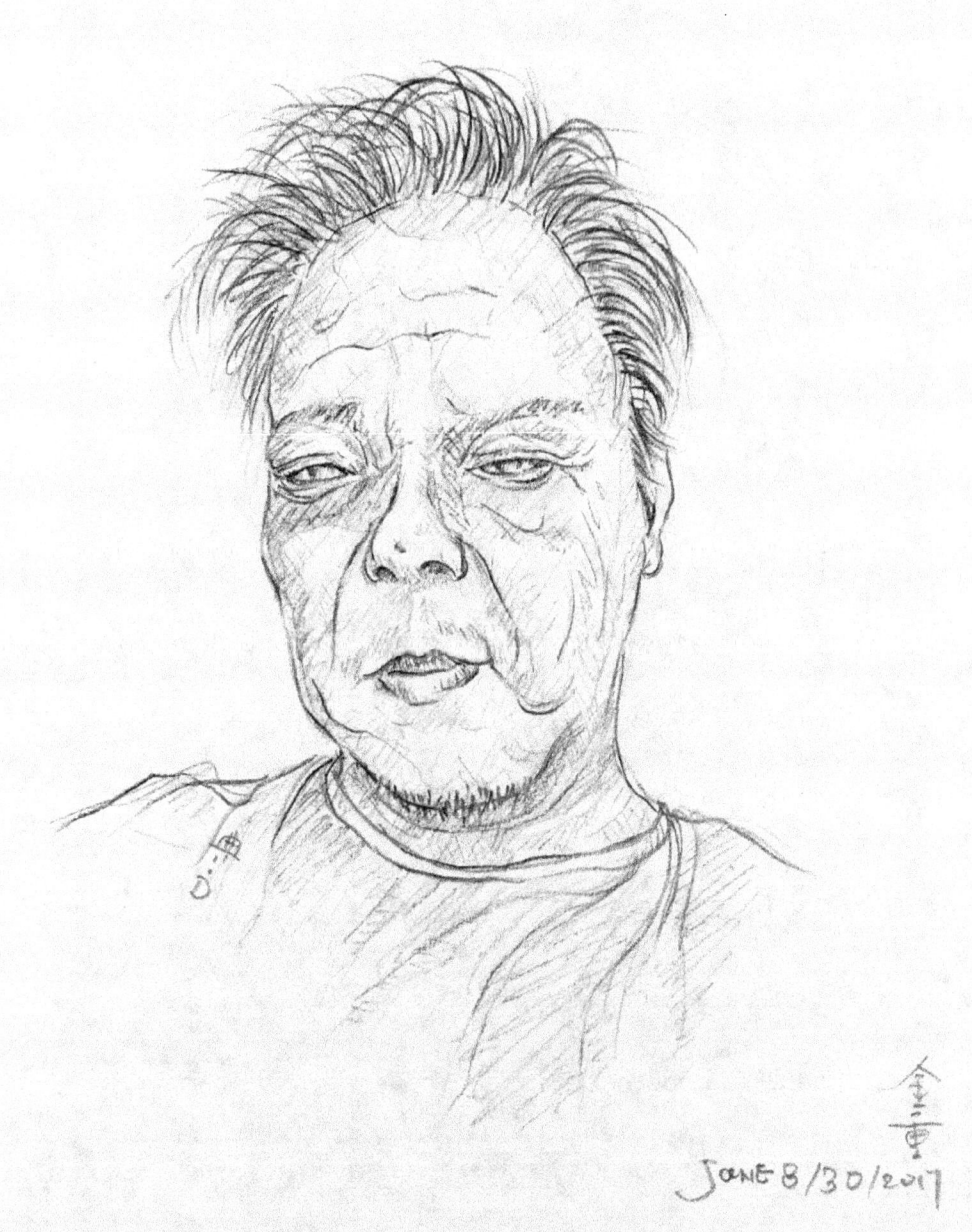

Jane 8/30/2017

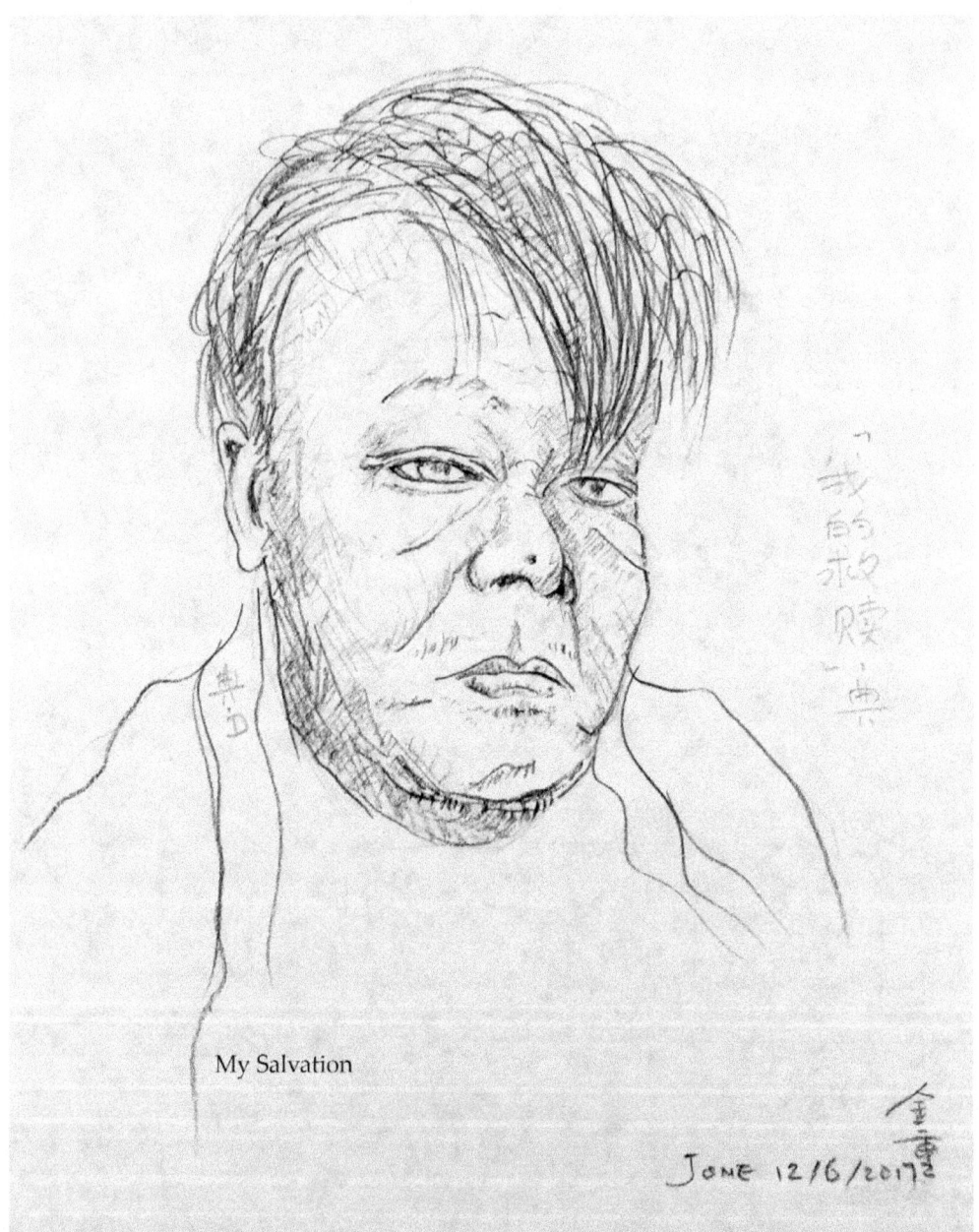

My Salvation

「我的救贖」畫

金重

Jone 12/6/2017

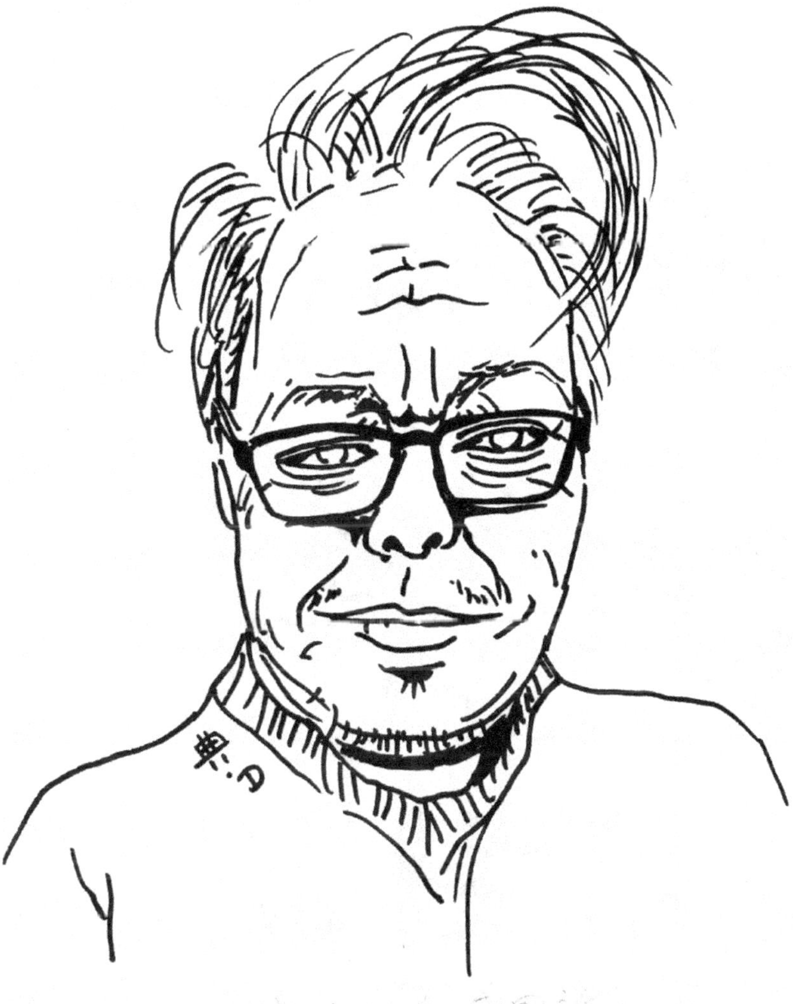

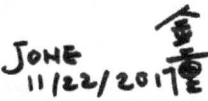

Thanksgiving
No idea who I should give my thanks to

JONE
11/22/2017

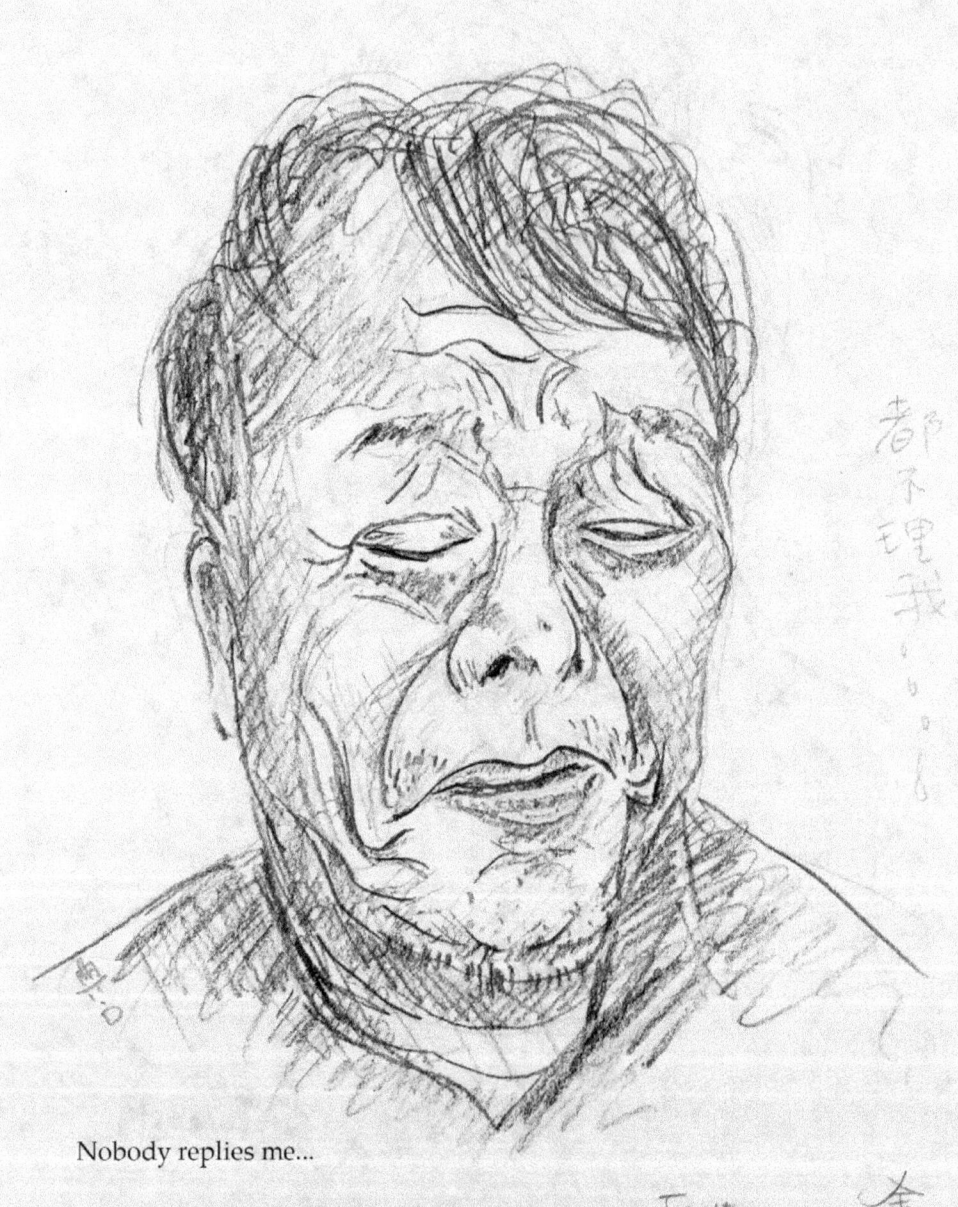

都不理我。。。

Nobody replies me...

JeNG
12/14/2017 金童

ICICLES

By Dian Qiu

Always wish

You write me something

Like snow falling onto the branches

But it doesn't snow in your world

Doesn't matter how cold it gets

If I ask again

You will hang a few icicles

From the eaves of my home

Translated by Jin Zhong

冰凌

典裘 作

总想你写点什么给我
就像枝头上飘落着一些雪
你的世界不再下雪
那怕再冷
最多结些冰凌
挂在我的屋檐

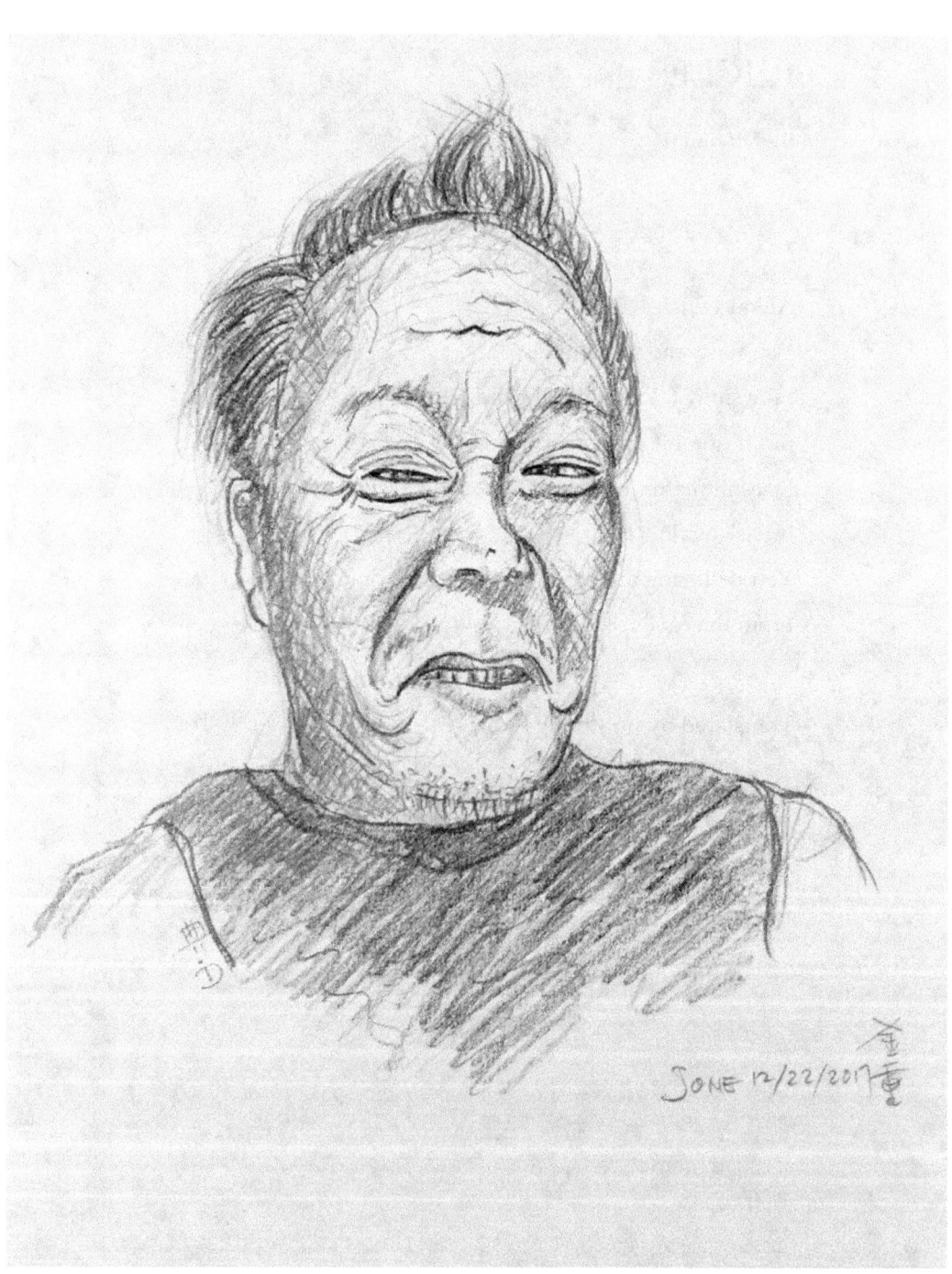

JONE 12/22/2017

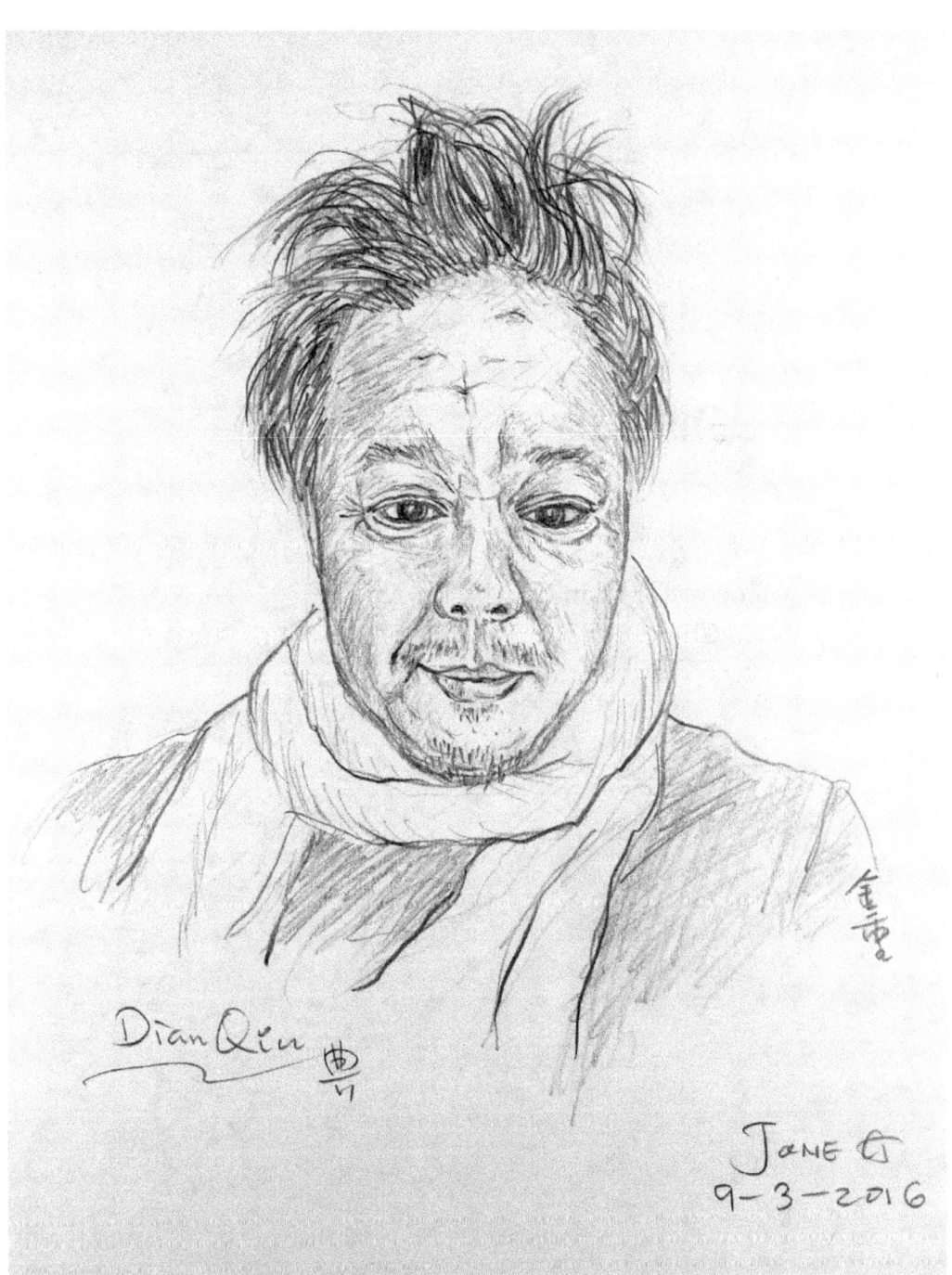

DianQiu 邮7

JANE G
9-3-2016

BONUS:

Poems for Dian Qiu, by Jin Zhong
(In Chinese)
金重写给典裘沽酒的诗歌

诗人钟结者典裘沽酒

本来诗人是个高尚的称呼
提起诗歌，人们自然想到
唐诗宋词，想起在水一方
但自从上个世纪八十年代以后
诗人的名声开始变坏
越变越坏
诗人的第一形象就是牛逼分子
天老大他老二
甚至他就是老大比天子还大
诗人的第二形象就是
满脸胡子满头脏发
一星期不洗澡一个月不换裤衩
诗人的第三形象就是穷酸的秀才
肩不能担担手不能提篮
五谷不分六亲不认
诗人的第四形象就是书房如同灵堂
供着各种大师的祖宗牌位
庞德艾略特萨特尼采应有尽有
诗人的第五形象就是神经病
走火入魔玩失踪玩跳江玩卧轨
你一提诗歌他就三高他就爆炸
八十年代的诗集一印就是几万册
如今没有出版社出资印任何诗集
连一千册都卖不掉！
人们早已不把诗歌视为神圣
人们早已不把诗人当做人看
只有诗人自己还继续觉得是人上人
是劳心者治人劳力者治于人
他们行贿受贿他们出卖肉体
他们鸡鸣狗盗欺骗大众骗取钱财
他们实际上和邪教已经没什么两样
他们霸山为王是新牛的赤壁之贼
难怪一位诗人在母亲节哀唱：
祖国母亲啊，为什么
这满街跑的都是王八蛋
这个诗族真的到了最危亡的时刻
这个诗歌的国度已魔鬼横行
就要毁于一个旦

"谁牛逼我就操谁！"
有人突然呐喊一声
所有的以上的那些诗人
都闭上了嘴巴
没有一个敢上前和这人叫板
这人就叫典裘沽酒
他突然在诗人的人海来了个硬着陆
火车被他撞出了轨
轮船被他弄翻了船
典裘以毒攻毒比毒药和毒品还毒
他的黄诗比乾隆的皇袍还黄
他的红诗比城楼还红
他的绿诗过绿了陈光标
你牛逼我正好廿你
你脏兮兮我比你还兮兮
你穷酸我比你酸一百倍
酸到叫你们满地找牙哭天喊地
你们摆灵堂我就撬开鲁迅的棺材
我就和梅 xx 做爱做出血染的风采
典裘是钟馗来到这庞大的诗国
诗鬼们闻风丧胆四散奔逃
第一个被钟结的是大今天的大主编
典裘给他扔下一颗大号的子弹壳
上面印着"通向地狱的通行证"
随后不管死鬼活鬼皆被钟结
典裘枪枪毙名弹不虚发
刚刚被钟结的是个叫金重的家伙
他虽然没有什么名气
但苗头很猛
很可能成为新的纳粹和独裁
必须被扼杀在摇篮之中
这家伙太狂妄
硬撑画画老师是鼻祖
硬撑文学老师是泰斗
硬撑自己是最后的流亡者
还成天秀他幸存者村庄的
海景屋和宝马
最要命的是他已学会了
典裘的后朦胧暗喻杀手锏
以及用深度中国文化编织先锋语言
还有七十二变的风格修辞
这小子简直太坏了
这小子太善于学习了

就算他在大洋彼岸
我典庖也不会放过他
不钟结他诗国将继续一潭浑水
不钟结他将为时太晚
不钟结他近期难以扫平天下

美国圣地亚哥。2016/4/6.

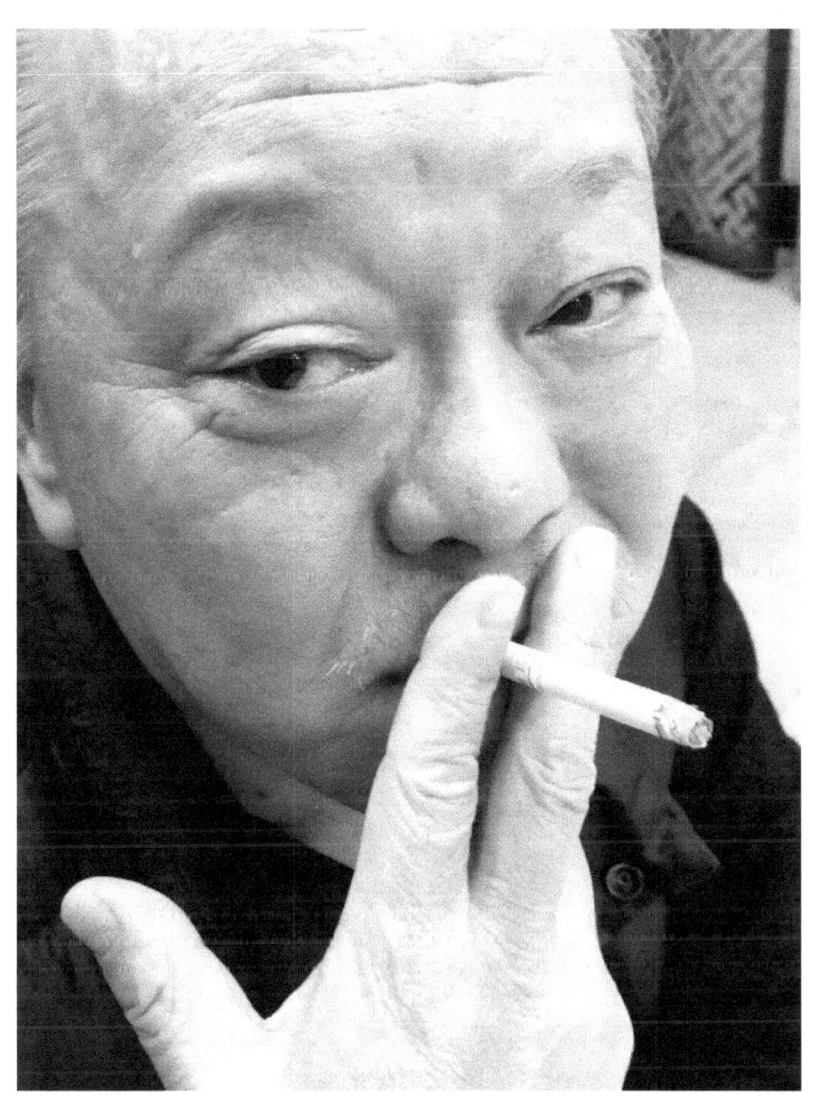

分歧

一条路分成两条平行的路
诗人们争吵后也分成两队

一队走 A 路，一队走 B 路
中间隔条山涧

走着走着
A 队就开始谴责 B 队
"你们走错了，要迷途知返！"

B 队也大喊：
"是你们走错了，迷途知返吧！"

双方一开始还算文明
不久就开始破口大骂

大家骂一骂停一停
一边继续向前走

这时典裘驾着轰炸机
飞到这两条路的上空：

"报告，发现目标
但不知攻击 A 路还是 B 路"

"请看前方，哪一条没有出路
就攻击哪条"

"Roger"典裘回答
随后投下重磅垃圾派炸弹

2016/9/20
注：Roger，美军通讯用的口语，表示已收到命令。

放了典裘吧

尊敬的领导大人：

典裘是个老顽童
喝酒爱高
见女人爱搞
有作风问题
但绝对没政治问题
实际上他是个维稳的神器
一夫胜过百万大军
一定要放老典回家啊
只要他在线读诗
人们就不会走上街头
老典一首诗
就能把千万人拴在手机上
街上万人空巷
下水道都空空荡荡
欺诈信息全部消失
雾霾雾霭不治而愈

天下因此而鸡宁犬静太平天国兮

金重敬上
2016-4-14

典右派的零分作文

典裘把稿子交给总编
总编在上面画个圈
典裘以为总编同意发表了
结果他把稿子扔进废纸篓

典裘把稿子交给评论家
评论家在上面画个圈
典裘以为评论家同意写文章了
结果他把稿子扔进了火炉子

典裘把稿子交给诗歌奖评委
评委在上面画了一个圈
典裘以为这次他要得奖了
结果评委把稿子从窗户撒了出去

典裘一怒之下把稿子发在了微通上
结果网友评论变成零
转发次数也转成零
随后账号也显示了一个大零蛋

2017

老典呐喊

一个大屋子
充满了狂欢的诗人
老典跳到台上
拼命呐喊
却没人听见
最后老典 ping 地一声
朝天花板开了一枪
红色天花板啪嚓掉下一大块
所有男男女女一下子静了下来
但不到一秒钟
就四散奔逃

老典说：真快！
比鸡都快！

2014

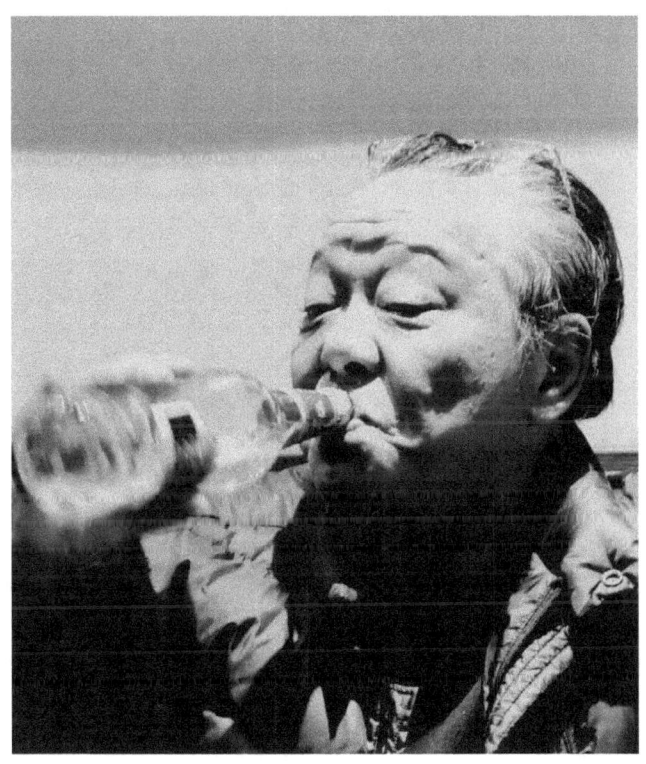

阐释典裘沽酒

一看到这个标题，许多人肯定厌倦
你为何天天画典裘写典裘，不能干点儿别的吗？

对不起，如果我扫了你的兴致
但我自己却是兴致勃勃！

海上菲十分好奇：学院派的金重为何能和垃圾派典裘
打的火热，这个值得当今诗歌界研究

典裘回答他的众多粉丝：金重是美国的翻译家，画家
诗歌是"知识分子写作"

不是的。想阐释典裘沽酒，我必须澄清一下自己：
我不是学院派，更不是知识分子写作

早在一九八九年，我在北京外国语学院研究生毕业后
就被王福祥院长开除，从此再无法踏入学院之门

被开除后在北京四处找工作，到处碰壁
同时王院长下令让保卫处对我连夜迫害审讯，追杀

我不得不离开中国流浪到美利坚
我在这里告诉大家：在美国 25 年我读过的文学书

加一起不到一百本。 我出版过的东西
加一起不到一本书----这算什么知识分子写作？

阐释典裘沽酒，起源于布罗茨基的一首诗
叫做阐释了的柏拉图，1988 年王伟庆翻译

因为世界文学发表了他的译作，王伟庆名扬了天下
所以，我阐释典裘沽酒

即使我不能名扬天下， 典裘沽酒也必定名扬天下
引用典裘的话：臭名昭著又何妨兮！

摆脱了学派的束缚，摆脱了名誉的囹圄
哈哈我跑掉了！这也是典裘垃圾诗歌的真正目的

引用高更的一句话：
D'où Venons Nous / Que Sommes Nous / Où Allons Nous

人们翻译成：我们从何处来？我们是谁？我们向何处去？
翻译错了

我认为应该翻译成：
我们是从什么地方来的？我们是什么东西？我们要去哪里？

继莎士比亚的"是生，还是死？"之后
高更的这句话是学院和知识分子们最爱夸夸"奇谈"的话题

啊，多么伟大的艺术，多么崇高的标题！
是的。没错。但是，你们在这里打转转没有任何意义

那么谁配谈论这"伟大"的标题？ 不是我。是典裘沽酒
他的众多作品已经告诉你：

你们是从哪里来的，你们是什么东西，你们要到哪里去
所以我找到了阐释典裘沽酒的最佳途径：

我说："我们从乌龟岛来，我们是乌龟，我们要去乌龟岛"
典裘说：不行，不够垃圾！

我说："我们从王八岛来，我们是王八，我们要去王八岛"
典裘说："你把我的垃圾诗歌理解错了！"

我说："我们从鸟岛来，我们是鸟，我们要去鸟岛！"
典裘高兴得蹦了起来： 这就对了！

2016，6，18.

中秋节我要去广州过

首先想到的是广州那几位美女诗人
到广州后马上去拜访一下
可想起老典那句话——
"那是人家的媳妇"
我摇摇头，就算了吧
那就去找赵俊杰这个纯爷们
可一进他的公司
就会被十几只美女的眼睛盯上
我摇摇头，这也算了吧
那就去我那个表亲的宿舍
可一想那是军队大院
弄不好我会被当作美国来的特务
还是自己去住酒店吧！
这样简单又清净
可人家说半夜就会有明妓暗娼来访
随后就有警察破门而入
就是没有警察
也会有各种骗子
冒充保安冒充城管冒充修电话的
总之你防不胜防
最后实在没办法
我还是住老典家吧
可典嫂一定会当我面
把典裘修理个半死
所以，我就住典裘的值班室吧！
那个值班室是平房
非常的方便还可以出门看看月亮
那一张木头长椅我就可以睡一宿
典裘还可以随地泼水
上次泼出个徐悲鸿的木马
这次说不定会泼出个嫦娥子
我说老典啊你随便泼一下就是大师之作
老典说我操你给我写的诗随便拿一首都能获撸迅文学奖
你看这值班室有多安全啊
外面的坏事情都不会发生在这里！
我说典哥啊我就有一个请求
告诉你手下的弟兄们
这中秋节的晚上
千万不要把那些人带进值班室
什么小偷大盗嫖客妓女
什么微信诈骗电话诈骗
什么人贩子狗贩子牛逼贩子
什么贪官污吏猪毛龟孙子

致命的秋天

我要到圣地亚哥城里
去画典裘
用白色蓝色和红色的大号粉笔
画出鲜明的大幅典裘
画出自由的典裘
画出爱情的典裘
画出呐喊的典裘
我要在路面上画
我要在大楼的高墙上画
我要在市政府纪念碑上画
我要在太平洋舰队的大门上画
直到警察或宪兵把我抓起来
我不在乎
我被指控成什么
新纳粹
恐怖组织
还是新共工党
或是直接把我关进
人满为患的
加利福尼亚疯人院

2016/10/4

@典裘

我发什么都爱@一下老典
发首诗
@一下老典
发张画
@一下老典
发张美图
也@一下老典
可典裘是个狱警啊
我@一下
就等于报了一次警

2017/9/13

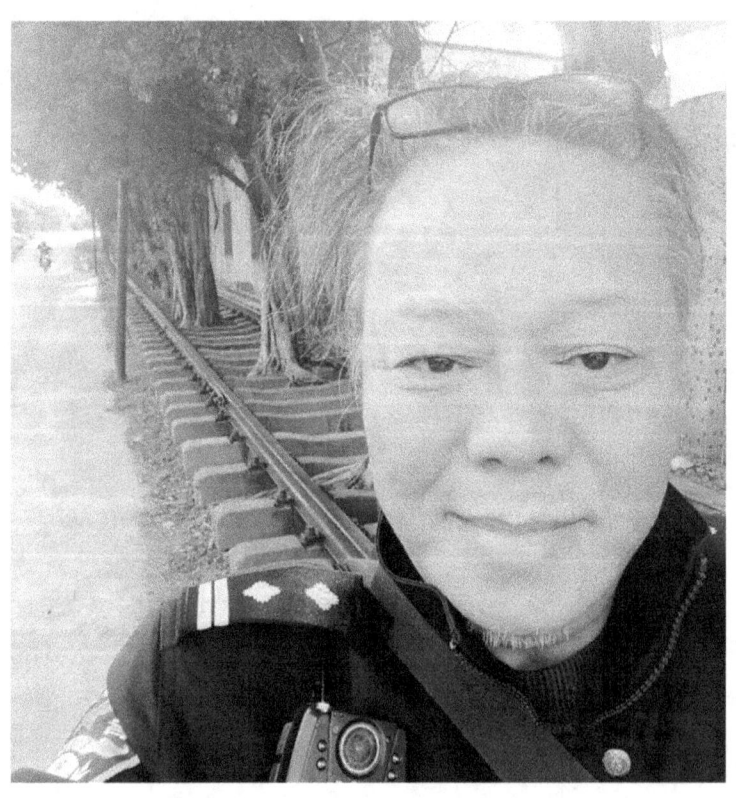

美利坚版诗行天下
《牛系列-15》

这么多糖果
吃不尽的糖果
各种各样的味道
有柠檬，芒果
有苹果，橘子
有草莓，香蕉
有西瓜，罂粟......
多情的女人
悲哀的女人
失恋的女人
不幸福的女人
离婚的女人
都爱来这里品尝、购买
如同品尝、购买
典裘沽酒的
爱情

2017-8-27
蒙特利糖果厂

美利坚版诗行天下
《牛系列-7》

这个奇特的地热喷泉
叫做柯蕾普赛得拉
它常年喷发
从不间歇

到了严寒的冬天
野牦牛都会来到这里
它们静静地站立
围绕着柯蕾普赛得拉取暖
就如同围绕着
典裘沽酒的爱情

2017-8-23
黄石公园

寻欢作乐

女囚管典裘叫正府
她总爱说：
正府好帅，真帅

典裘撒了一个谎
说自己是单身
被女囚识破
于是典裘撒了一个更大的慌
说自己离婚了

女囚说：
你怎么跟我撒谎啊，正府？
典裘瞧了瞧她的屁股说：
你的裤子漏了一个洞
我当然要用一块
比洞还大的布丁去补嘛！

女囚笑了
露出一口整洁的白牙：
你真不要脸

2017，2

天问

啪！
啪！
啪！
梅导演敲了三下桌子
乱哄哄的诗人们
静了下来

"老典，你一定记住了
跳江时一定不要 DIVE
不要扎猛子
这水才半米深！"

"诗人们，你们扔粽子
千万别砸到老典的头！"

"听-清-啦！"
大家一起回答

红色帷幕缓缓拉开
一束聚光灯
投在老典饱经沧桑的脸上

受寿永多，夫何久长？
中央共牧，后何怒？
蜂蛾微命，力何固？
本无苍天，天何问？

观众突然爆发
雷鸣般的掌声

梅导演急了：
老典，错啦！
你他妈的疯了！

这时老典跑到江边
开始脱鞋

梅导演大喊：
准备好粽子

他要投江啦！

诗人们一手紧抓一个肉粽子
心里都要砸老典

老典把衣服脱个精光
开始沿江裸奔

梅导演抓起喇叭：
我操！
快跳哇！你到是跳哇！

老典魔怔了
根本不去跳江
而是向观众跑去！

一些观众目瞪口呆
一些观众捂上眼睛

他边跑边喊：
"灭亡啦！楚国灭了！
终于灭啦！"

端午快乐！2016

铸典裘

我要铸造
十个青铜典裘
用伟大诗人典裘的原型
身高一米七四
纷乱的头发
消瘦、哀伤的脸庞
每个手里
都捧着一本诗集
像捧着一本
祈祷的经书
十个典裘
一个身穿学生服
一个身穿教授服
一个身穿工作服
一个身穿医生服
一个身穿警察服
一个身穿环保卫服
一个身穿运动服
一个身穿大厨服
一个身穿邮差服
一个身穿铁路服

十个典裘
我要赠给未来的北京城
把它们放在汽车站旁
让所有上下班的人们
让所有去天安门的中外游客
都看到伟大的典裘
第十个，放在公主坟
第九个，放在军事博物馆
第八个，放在木樨地
就这样，一直放到天安门

2016/10/8

这家超市

我最爱
来这家超市
因为它边上
有一小火车站

站台再小
也是站台
典裘说
火车再小
也有爱情

2017/1/29

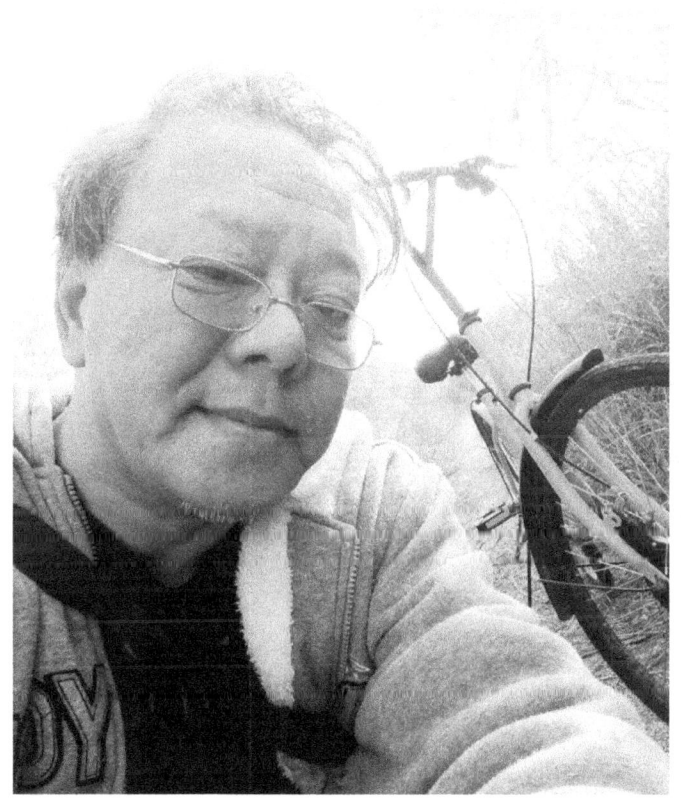

给典裘沽酒的同伴

警察先生
你们不要扫黄
要扫
就去扫红
去扫那滚滚红尘
留下
我们月淡星稀
柳垂晓塘的
风尘

2016/6

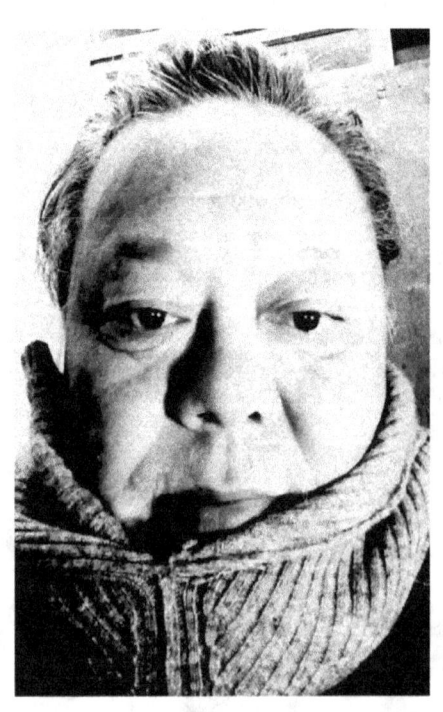

老典我要为你举办巴黎广场《呐喊》诗歌朗诵会

当年的手提喇叭交给你
当年的"自由万岁"交给你
当年人山人海的呼应交给你
当年的百盏华灯交给你
当年的一万面旗帜交给你--

呐喊，老典！穿上你的五四长袍
戴上你的五四长围脖
双手展开你写在报纸上的诗篇
站立在雪白的大理石的台阶上
呐！喊！

今天五四--广场属于人民
今天五四--广场属于共和国
今天五四—广场属于法兰西
今天五四--广场属于你和我
今天你告诉人们这些鲜花究竟是在哀悼谁
今天你告诉人们谁才是人民的英雄
呐喊！呐喊是摧毁撒旦的装甲
呐喊是摧毁纳粹的火山
呐喊--你是历史枪膛里的达姆弹

今夜整个世界都在注视巴黎广场
今夜埃菲尔铁塔上
中法双语《呐喊》和《LIBERTÉ》的激光交替辉映
一百万只手机同时亮起如自由之火遍地燎原
一百万个喉咙排山倒海呼应你的呐喊

2016，5，4，晚7：40-8：00

典裘沽酒得到了缪斯的眷顾

赵俊杰

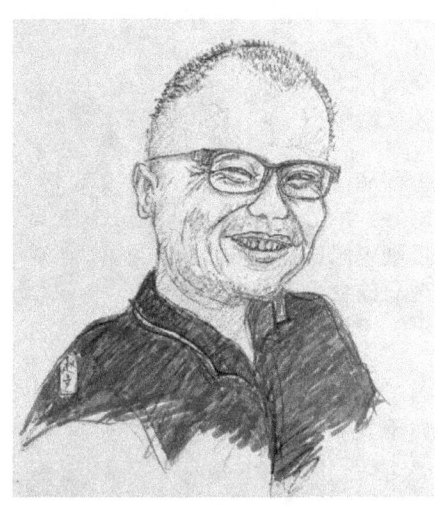

有时老典自己都说，真他妈的幸运，金重为他画了三百幅肖像画。

问金重，为什么要给老典画这么多？金重说闲得无聊。那你闲得无聊怎么不给张三李四王五赵六画？为什么非得给老典画了一张又一张？说来说去，还是受到了老典的"魅惑"！老典的确是个比女人还好玩的人，他的搞怪，他的诙谐，他的恶习，他的各种坏毛病，都是好玩的材料。连黑他的梅老邪有时也不得不这么感慨！

老典是真诗人的性情，这里需要搞清楚一个问题：什么叫真诗人？我们在教科书上看到的诗人总是千人一面的一副学富五车、严于律己的榜样，是这样吗？或者说真诗人只有这单一的类型吗？事实上很多特别牛逼的诗人就是"流氓+神棍"。你别不信，我们来看李白和杜甫，可能会给大家带来一些启示。李白不只是诗写得好，天纵之才，你看他的玩法，连唐玄宗的老婆杨贵妃都敢调戏。这事如果发生在今天，会被以道德自居的诗人们的口水淹死。再来看杜甫，他在秩秩大国大唐竟然写"朱门酒肉臭，路有冻死骨"这种描写社会黑暗的诗，如果这诗出现在当今，诗人们怎么来看？陈傻子、未满、啊昌、走召写批判作品被猛烈抨击就是是好的答案。老典就是这种类型的诗人，他放浪形骸，招摇过市，纵酒朗诵，不管不顾，只在快活，也许，正是这些"毛病"让老典得以完全坦露，让画家金重看到了一个戏剧性、有残缺、多角度的诗人典裘沽酒，这就是能让他一直画下来的理由。

金重是非常了解老典的性格的，他甚至用他的笔揭示了老典内心的顽劣和阴影（借这个机会，我也提出希望老典能改掉些臭毛病）。他画老典，有时将他比作一头肥猪、一条蟒蛇、一头公牛、一条鱼，或是一辆坦客、一艘飞船……好了，大家来看金重是怎么来画老典的吧。

www.ingramcontent.com/pod-product-compliance
Lightning Source LLC
Chambersburg PA
CBHW081728220526

45468CB00008B/2014